ABOUT THE AUTHOR

Siobhan Curham is an award-winning author, motivational speaker and life coach. Her books for adults are: *Dare to Write a Novel*, *True Love Always*, *The Sweet Revenge of the Football Widows*, *The Scene Stealers* and *Antenatal & Postnatal Depression*. Her books for young adults include *Dear Dylan* (winner of the Young Minds Book Award), *True Face*, *The Moonlight Dreamers* series and *Don't Stop Thinking About Tomorrow*. Siobhan has written for many newspapers, magazines and websites, including the *Guardian*, *Cosmopolitan*, *Mother and Baby*, *Practical Parenting* and *Take a Break*. She has also been a guest on various radio and TV shows, including Woman's Hour, BBC News, GMTV and BBC Breakfast. Find out more at www.siobhancurham.com and on Instagram @spiritualmisfits.

SOMETHING MORE

. . . A SPIRITUAL MISFIT'S SEARCH FOR MEANING

SIOBHAN CURHAM

piatkus

PIATKUS

First published in Great Britain in 2019 by Piatkus

1 3 5 7 9 10 8 6 4 2

A CIP catalogue record for this book
is available from the British Library.

ISBN 978-0-349-42083-7

Typeset in Garamond by M Rules
Printed and bound in Great Britain by
Clays Ltd, Elcograf S.p.A.

Papers used by Piatkus are from well-managed forests
and other responsible sources.

For Michael Curham . . . my life and this book
wouldn't be nearly as rich and wise
without you in it. Namaste!

Make your own bible. Select and collect all the words and sentences that in all your readings have been to you like the blast of a trumpet.

RALPH WALDO EMERSON

CONTENTS

Introduction   1

1   Signs of Something More   5

2   Chanting up a Storm with the
    Buddhists   15

3   What Would Jesus Do?   25

4   The Power of Prayer   37

5   Saintly Sexism   53

6   Sacred Feminine   67

7   Divine Dance Class   83

8   From Wonder to Gratitude   95

9   Manifesting Abundance . . . and
    False Gurus   107

10 Tuning in to Tarot   123

11 Yoga, Death and Downward Dogs   137

12 Don't Reiki and Drive   149

13 Finding My Shamanic
    Animal Guide   159

14 Going on Retreat   169

15 Pilgrimages to Thin Places   181

16 Soulmates and Soul Friends   189

17 Mindfulness and Thinking
    Yourself Happy   203

18 Spiritual Tools for Tough Times   213

19 Forgive the Fooker   229

    In the End . . .   239

INTRODUCTION

In 2017 something momentous happened: a British Attitudes Survey showed that for the first time, the majority of people living in the UK (53 per cent) didn't belong to a religion. Another study has shown that only 1.4 per cent of the population now attend an Anglican Church service on a Sunday morning. This shift away from the Church isn't unique to the UK. Between 1979 and 2011 the number of Roman Catholics attending a weekly church service in Ireland fell from 91 per cent to 30 per cent, and a 2015 survey showed that only 15 per cent of Irish Anglicans attend a Sunday service. A similar decline is happening on the other side of the Atlantic. Various studies have shown that less than 20 per cent of Americans now attend church services and in 2013, Southern Baptist researcher Thom Rainer estimated that between 8,000 and 10,000 churches were likely to close that year.

However, the hordes of people turning their backs on religion aren't necessarily turning their backs on spirituality. In fact, a growing number of people (20 per cent in the UK and 25 per cent in the US) now refer to themselves as 'spiritual but not reli-gious'. This book is for those people – the ones who, for whatever reason, have turned away from or could never relate to religion, but still believe there's Something More to this thing called life; people who desire a spiritual anchor in what is becoming an ever more turbulent and fast-paced world. I am one of those people. Having been raised as a devout atheist, in 2011 I set out on a quest to see if there was anything in this spiritual business – if it could bring me a lasting source of strength, love and joy that had so far eluded me. Although I knew next to nothing about reli-gion and spirituality, I had had two experiences at rock-bottom moments in my life when I'd inexplicably felt the presence of something far greater than me.

My quest to find out what this 'something' was took me down some fascinating, unexpected and occasionally hilarious paths. Over a seven-year period I chanted up a storm with Buddhists, joined – and promptly left – a Christian church, fell foul of a false guru, studied the teachings of ancient Jewish scholars and the poetry of the Sufis, danced with the divine, tuned in to my inner goddess, had a passionate encounter with a soulmate and made true soul friends. I took part in a Mayan cacao ceremony and ended up talking to trees, met my shamanic spirit animal and had part of my soul retrieved. I also studied mindfulness and became a Reiki-healer-tarot-reader and much, much more. In short, my exploration of different spiritual traditions was a revelation to a devout atheist like me.

Once I cut through the dogma that had put me off before, I found certain teachings and practices that I've come to view as superpowers, beautiful in their simplicity. They form the basis of my life today – the basis of my inner joy, strength and peace, and the basis of this book. This book is for spiritual misfits like me, who have had enough of the doctrine of separation and fear. It is for those who look around at the world today – at the politics of division, the hashtags of hate and the spiralling mental health crisis – and think, *surely there has to be a better way?*

Numerous scientific studies are now showing the benefits of a spiritual practice. In an article titled 'The neuroscience of spirituality and religion', William Sears MD, a doctor with fifty years' experience, says that science has now shown beyond doubt that spiritual people have 'happier brains, healthier bodies and longer lifespans'. Focusing on something greater than ourselves and on a sense of connection with others helps lift us out of negative thinking. Pathways are created in the brain that enhance our sense of self and our empathy. Studies have also shown that a regular meditation practice reduces blood pressure, stress and anxiety, and boosts our immunity. Neuro-imaging techniques have shown that meditation stimulates the brain's compassion centre. Mindfulness also has a calming effect on the amygdala, the part of the brain that produces fear responses. Sears concludes his article by urging everyone to make a spiritual practice part of their health routine.

So, if the word 'religion' sends you running to your collected works of Dawkins muttering, 'Out-of-date mumbo jumbo,' I would urge you to take a small step rather than a giant leap of faith, and invest a few hours reading these pages, absorbing the lessons I've learnt and trying the practices I recommend. This is a book about finding deep inner joy and peace, and most of all, a love that unites and guides instead of divides; a love that doesn't care if you're male, female, straight, gay, black, white or purple; a love that frees us from fear and revolutionises the way we view ourselves, each other and the world.

1

SIGNS OF SOMETHING MORE

All shall be well.

JULIAN OF NORWICH

In the beginning (in *my* beginning) was the Word, and the Word was with atheism and the Word was atheism. Both my parents had been brought up in religious families (my father, Catholic, my mother, Protestant) and both rebelled against their religions in their teens. When my parents got married (in a religion-free register office, naturally) they agreed that there was no way any children of theirs would have to endure enforced Sunday school or weekly confession. Instead, we would be left entirely free to choose our own faith, if we so wished, once we'd reached an age when we were able to make such an important decision. However, this wasn't quite how it turned out. Rather than being brought up neutrally – in a 'spiritual Switzerland', if you like – my three siblings and I were brought up to see the Church as something to be avoided at all costs. In our house, religion and capitalism were seen as twin evils, designed to indoctrinate and oppress. When I became a Girl Guide I was banned from going to church parades on Sundays, the way other children might be banned from taking drugs or from talking to strangers. My parents even discussed forbidding me to attend school assembly. This horrified me – not because I particularly enjoyed having to sit cross-legged on a cold hall floor singing 'Morning Has Broken' for what felt like hours on end, but because there was only one other person who was banned from going to assembly. She was a Jehovah's Witness and as every kid in our playground knew, Jehovah's Witnesses didn't agree with blood transfusions and therefore *believed in letting sick babies die.* If my mum and dad banned me from going to assembly, people would think that I killed babies too, or so my panic-stricken eight-year-old self thought. Thankfully, after much begging and pleading on my part, they succumbed.

Of course, as a result of all this 'just say no to religion', the Church took on a hugely elicit thrill to me. I craved Sunday school the way other kids craved sweets. And when my Catholic best friend had to go to her first confession I was eaten up with envy. The thought of sitting in a velvet-curtained box with an unseen priest, fessing up to how you'd stolen your little brother's Action Man figure and drawn rude pictures on its naked body seemed so dramatic and exciting. Why couldn't I be a sinner too? One day, on the way home from school, I found a small cruci-fix pendant on the pavement. I smuggled it into my bedroom and hid it with a photo of my grandad Bob inside an envelope marked 'Private. Keep out!' – which as any savvy child knows, is *guaranteed* to ward off prying parental eyes. This envelope became my secret link to the divine – well, kind of. At night I would take the crucifix and photo from the envelope, carefully place them on my pillow and say a prayer to Grandad Bob. He had died earlier that year and had been a deeply religious man. He'd kept a bottle of holy water by his front door and went to mass every single day. He was the closest thing to Jesus I'd known so I prayed to him – usually about some terrible transgression my parents had made, or asking if he could help me sort out a friendship drama.

However, by the time I reached my teens and my parents' marriage had broken up, my resulting disillusionment at the world took in everything, including God. I binned my holy envelope and stopped praying to Grandad Bob. *Religion is the opiate of the masses*, I'd think to myself without a hint of irony, as I bunked off school to get stoned in a friend's flat. Even when I became an adult and mellowed a bit, I still avoided church like the plague. After growing up on a news diet of 'The Troubles' in Northern Ireland and, more recently, 'The Global War on Terror', religions had become inextricably linked to conflict in my mind. They also seemed way out of touch when it came to issues like women and sexuality. But then I had the first of what I now refer to as my 'Something More moments'.

I'd just turned thirty, was mum to a young son and my marriage had taken a very dark turn for the worse. I spent every day and most nights plagued by fear and riddled with anxiety. I'd started having panic attacks, and my despair that I'd never be able to escape my situation had begun manifesting as self-harm. One cold winter's night, when I was out with my husband and a friend, the issues in our marriage, which had until then been hidden like a dirty secret within the four walls of our home, became public in the most humiliating way imaginable.

As I trudged home through the icy fog that night, feeling

lower than I'd ever felt before, something strange happened. I was suddenly and dramatically lifted from my despair. *It doesn't get any worse than this*, an inner voice told me. But instead of this seeming a bad thing, I felt strangely reassured. *It doesn't get any worse than this, so therefore it has to get better. It has to get better and it will.* I had no idea where this inner voice and its resulting feeling of peace and calm was coming from, but I let it fill me. The next morning I told my dad the truth about my relationship. He stared at me across the table, a horrible montage of shock, anger and sorrow playing out upon his face. Finally he spoke, his voice deadly serious.

'No one should have to live like this. *You* should not have to live like this.' The curse of silence, fear and shame I'd been living under had finally been broken.

It took another few months for me to find the courage to end my marriage, but what happened to me that cold, dark night was the catalyst and I never forgot that strange sensation inside – and yet outside – of me. I never forgot how it reassured me that all would be well and gave me the impetus to break fear's spell.

I wouldn't experience this strange feeling again until some eight years later, when I was six years into a relationship with a guy called Steve. It was the middle of January, peak flu season, and Steve was taken seriously ill. What was at first wrongly diagnosed as the winter vomiting virus turned out to be a brain tumour, which turned out to be an extremely aggressive form of cancer. The day Steve had to have life-saving – and life-threatening – surgery to remove the brain tumour, I was distraught. Unsure that I'd ever see him again, fear floored me. The hospital he was having surgery in was right around the corner from Great Ormond Street – a specialist hospital for children in central London. My sister had been to Great Ormond Street many times and she'd told me that if it all got too much I should visit the chapel there as she'd always found it somewhere peaceful to escape to. Now, at this point in my life, I was still in my 'religion is the opiate of the masses' phase and hadn't set foot in a church apart from for the occasional wedding. But as I waited for the outcome of what I'd been told would be an extremely lengthy surgical procedure, I was desperate – so much so that I found myself stumbling into Great Ormond Street and following the signs to the chapel. The first thing that hit me when I walked in were the cuddly toys. Soft and furry and every colour of the rainbow, they lined a shelf all around the wall. The sight of them was strangely reassuring. I sat down on a polished wooden pew and, for the first time since my holy envelope days, I began to pray – really pray. It was a very short and simple prayer, consisting mainly of one word: 'Please'.

Please make it go OK. Please let him be OK. Please don't let him die. Over and over again. Then, all of a sudden, my fear was gone, replaced by the most beautiful sense of calm and knowing. *It's all going to be OK.* Just as on that cold dark night that had signalled the beginning of the end of my marriage, this voice and this knowing seemed to come from a place deep within me but it wasn't *of* me. Or at least, it bore no resemblance to my normal inner voice and its rolling script of fear. *It's all going to be OK.* I sat there for a while, bathing in the stillness, the warmth and the certainty. Then I got up and went to a cafe, where I sat for a further few hours, drinking coffee, reading and knowing, just knowing, that it was all going to be OK. Eventually, I returned to the hospital to see how the surgery was going, even though a member of staff had recommended that I go home for the day as the operation would take so long.

'Oh, he's out of surgery,' the duty nurse told me. 'You can come and see him if you like.'

She took me through the Intensive Care Unit, past a room marked 'Relatives', with an ominous box of tissues on the coffee table. And there was Steve, sitting up, smiling and singing football songs, off his head on morphine.

There's a line in the Leonard Cohen song 'Anthem' that perfectly sums up what I'm trying to describe here. It talks about a crack being needed for the light to get in. It's during our dark nights, or days, of the soul that something deep inside us cracks open, allowing a deeper understanding to slip in. Many people talk of having spiritual epiphanies when they hit rock bottom. A cancer diagnosis, the death of a loved one, a prison sentence, a job loss, a marriage break-up – all bring us to our knees and offer us the opportunity to sense that maybe, just maybe, there's something more at work here. Some people might choose to ignore these signs of Something More, some are instantly converted to a spiritual path, and others – like me – put them on the back-burner for a while, not exactly sure what to do with them.

I wrote the first draft of this chapter during a meeting of a writing group I belong to. When I read it to the other members of the group, one of them told me it reminded her of someone called Julian of Norwich and her famous quote: 'All shall be well, and all shall be well, and all manner of things shall be well.' I'd never heard of Julian of Norwich, so I made a mental note to investigate further. Less than an hour after the writing group ended, I was sitting in my kitchen and felt the sudden urge to flick through one of those advertising supplements that come with the Sunday papers. I never normally read these supplements – weirdly enough, I have no desire to own a china doll that 'looks just like a new-born baby' or a royal wedding commemorative plate. But as I opened the supplement at a random page, my eyes were drawn to a photo of a silver pendant inscribed with a quote. The caption above it read: 'Julian of Norwich, All Shall Be Well Pendant'. I mean, seriously, what are the chances?

I took this as a definite sign that I should investigate Julian of Norwich further, so I immediately consulted my trusty research assistant – Google. Here's what I found. Julian of Norwich was born in 1342 and was a Christian anchoress – someone who set themselves apart from society, devoting themselves entirely to God, and confining themselves to a cell attached to a church. There was a window in her cell that looked out into the church it joined on to. People would come to the window seeking spiritual advice, as if she were a hotline to God.

When Julian was thirty she became seriously ill – so ill that she had the last rites administered to her. She then experienced what today might be called a near-death experience, during which she had a series of spiritual revelations. In one of these, Jesus came to her and told her not to worry at all, reassuring her that: 'All shall be well, and all shall be well, and all manner of things shall be well.'

When Julian of Norwich recovered from her illness she vowed to be joyful in all circumstances, however dire, because she'd been shown and more importantly had *felt* a love that transcended all fear, and reassured her that all would be OK. Now it could be that if you're an atheist, you hold no truck with the concept of Jesus. But that doesn't matter. I believe that what matters here is what Julian of Norwich *felt* rather than how she saw or described it. It was the same transformative sense of reassurance and peace that I felt on that cold winter's night which signalled the beginning of the end of my marriage, and on that awful day Steve was having brain surgery. Julian of Norwich was a devout follower of Christ, so it makes sense to me that she should have seen Jesus as a symbol of love. It also makes sense to me that I didn't see Jesus when I had my own overwhelming sense that 'all shall be well'. I'd been a confirmed atheist my whole life.

We humans can get so hung up on needing to explain everything away with concepts, labels, stories and rules, but in this book I'd like to peel away those layers to look at what lies beneath. I think Julian of Norwich magically worked her way into these pages via my fellow writing group member and a Sunday supplement because she's proof that people have been experiencing this mysterious 'Something More' for centuries. We might attach different explanations to what happens in these moments in the darkness when the light pours in, but ultimately that deep knowing that 'all shall be well' is exactly the same. The question is, where does it come from?

Something More

All shall be well

Perhaps you've had a similar experience to mine. Maybe you once had a dark night of the soul and suddenly and for no apparent reason felt awash with peace or hope. Maybe your inner voice spoke to you with an authority or wisdom that felt alien to you, and although it was coming from within you, it was not of you. Take some time to reflect on how this made you feel. Or, if you're currently going through a difficult time, take some time to sit in silence and stillness and invite in that feeling. Don't force it, just be. If it helps, try repeating the mantra, 'All shall be well', silently or out loud. Make a note of what happens and how it makes you feel.*

---

* I recommend several written exercises in this book, so you might want to use a notebook as a 'Something More Journal', not only for these exercises but also to keep a record of any interesting thoughts or findings you make along the way. I feel fairly certain you'll experience quite a few.

2

CHANTING UP A STORM
WITH THE BUDDHISTS

Peace comes from within. Do not seek it without.

Gautama Buddha

Sadly, a year after Steve's recovery our relationship came to an end. It was an extremely loving end and to this day we remain the best of friends, but nonetheless I was heartbroken. My son and I were in desperate need of a fresh start, so I did the modern-day equivalent of sticking a pin in a map. I hovered my cursor over Google maps and found us a new home in a village in a completely different part of the country.

We arrived in the village in autumn 2010, exchanging the noise and grime of London for the fresh air and breathtaking landscape of the Chiltern Hills. The first night we were there I hated the pin-drop silence. After the constant London soundtrack of sirens, drunks and car horns, I found it unsettling.

That was soon to change. I quickly grew to love the tranquillity, which was broken only by the whistle of birdsong and the rustle of leaves. We lived in a tiny cottage overlooking a valley. At night the sky was velvety black and the stars shone like diamonds with no light pollution to dim them. Although our house didn't have an open fire most of the neighbours' homes did, and the fires perfumed the village with the sweet smell of wood smoke.

My son thrived in our new location, as did our dog. We'd got Max from a rescue centre and he'd always been jittery due to his previous owner's mistreatment. But now he had open fields to run around in he was transformed. And me? I felt myself relax and unwind with every cheek-glowing walk and starlit night. I'd always believed myself to be a city girl, but once the stunning landscape started seeping into my bones I never wanted to return to London life again.

After a few months of country bliss I had the idea to write a book on the secret of true happiness. It was something I'd always wanted to do as an extension of my motivational speaking and life coaching but there was just one small problem, which became a major problem when I sat down to write. While it was true that I was feeling a lot happier since moving, I certainly wasn't in any position to advise others on how to be happy. On many nights I cried myself to sleep. The main reason? Single at the age of forty, I felt like a failure romantically – a feeling that was exacerbated by some excruciating internet dating experiences. I'd read enough self-help books with cringey titles like *Women Who Love Tattooed Men Too Much* to know that I was looking for a romantic relationship to heal some kind of inner wound. I'd had enough counselling sessions to know that this inner wound had probably been caused by events in my childhood. But I was sick of blaming my parents. I was forty, for Christ's sake. Like wearing leather hot pants, parent blaming becomes slightly unsightly after a certain age. I decided that I couldn't write a book on finding true happiness until I'd actually found true happiness. The trouble was, I'd run out of places to look for it. Or had I?

Memories of my Something More moments had left huge question marks in my mind. Had they been some kind of spiritual experience? Did they hold the key to the inner peace that was eluding me? Did true happiness lie in spirituality? For the previous couple of years I'd witnessed a friend of mine undergo an incredible transformation. When I'd first met her she'd been plagued by health issues and unsure of what she wanted to do with her life. But subsequently she'd started to glow with vitality and had landed her dream job. The thing she credited most with her transformation was becoming a Buddhist. I was such a spiritual novice back then that I didn't know the first thing about Buddhism. I quickly did some background reading and discovered the following key facts:

- Buddhism began in India in around 500 BC.
- The word Buddha means 'the enlightened one'.
- Buddhism is based on the teachings of an Indian prince named Siddharta Guatama, who became known as the Buddha.
- Guatama was so shocked by the poverty and hardship he witnessed outside his palace that he gave up his life of luxury in order to find out how to eliminate human suffering.
- Eventually Guatama discovered the answer and spent the rest of his life teaching his findings.
- Buddha's teachings centre around Four Noble Truths:

1. Existence is suffering.
2. The cause of suffering is craving and attachment.
3. If we can give up our craving, suffering will cease and turn to Nirvana (bliss).
4. There is a path to Nirvana which is made up of eight steps, also known as the eight-fold path.

Buddhism, it turns out, has many different branches. My friend had chosen to follow a branch called Nichiren Buddhism. Nichiren was a thirteenth-century Buddhist monk from Japan. He believed that the mystic law which led to spiritual enlightenment was encapsulated in the Buddhist *Lotus Sutra* (one of the most important sacred scriptures in Buddhism). He named this law *Nam-myoho-renge-kyo*. The definition of this phrase can be broken down as follows:

Nam To devote or dedicate oneself.

Myo Mystic.

Ho Law.

Renge Lotus flower. The lotus flower is used because Buddhists believe that it symbolises the beauty of humanity in spite of the sufferings of daily life, just as the lotus blossom is untainted by the muddy waters in which it grows. The lotus also flowers and produces fruits at the same time, thereby symbolising the immediacy of the principle of cause and effect. Nichiren believed that we don't have to wait to bring forth the power of the mystic law, but can access it at any time.

Kyo Sutra or eternal truth.

So, put together, *Nam-myoho-renge-kyo* means to dedicate one-self to the mystic law of the *Lotus Sutra*.

The *Lotus Sutra*'s key message is that Buddhahood – the potential for limitless love, compassion, wisdom and cour-age – exists within all of us, regardless of race, sex, intelligence or class. Although it originated in Japan, there are now many followers of Nichiren Buddhism all over the world. The singer Tina Turner credits it with transforming her life for the better following her marriage break-up with Ike. Tina Turner and my friend, both transformed – perhaps there was something in this Nichiren Buddhist malarkey. Could it transform me for the better too?

A key practice in Nichiren Buddhism is chanting the mantra: 'Nam-myoho-renge-kyo'. When I expressed an interest in find-ing out more my friend slipped a piece of paper containing the mantra into my hand. 'Try chanting this every day and focus on what you'd like to achieve in your life,' she told me. I felt as if I'd been given the secret password to a magical kingdom. Part of me was excited ... and another part was deeply cynical. How could chanting some random words in Japanese possibly bring about true happiness? But I figured I had nothing to lose so I might as well give it a go.

One day when my son was at school – and all the windows were firmly closed – I sat cross-legged on a cushion and began chanting the words over and over again. Once my dog Max had got over his initial shock and stopped barking along with me, I started getting quite into it. I even created a little tune to sing the words to, to make it more enjoyable. As I sang 'Nam-myoho-renge-kyo' over and over again, I thought of all the things I'd like to achieve: success as a writer, enough money to live comfortably and, of course, a romantic relationship. There was something about the rhythm of the chant that really helped get me focused and, weirdly enough, I also felt quite empowered. Even though I was only sitting there sing-chanting and freaking out my dog, I felt as if I was actually doing something towards achieving my dreams. It felt good. So I began carving out some time each day to have a little sing-song on my cushion and focus in on my dreams. At the end of each session I'd feel energised and determined, and sometimes I'd get fresh ideas popping into my head where I'd previously been blocked. After a while I decided to take things a step further and got in touch with my local Nichiren Buddhist group. It turned out that it met in the street just behind mine. I wondered whether this could be a sign. Was this meant to be?

The first Nichiren Buddhist meeting I attended was hugely embarrassing on several counts. Firstly, I discovered that I'd been pronouncing the chant wrongly – completely wrongly. The only word I'd managed to say correctly was 'nam'. All the other words bore no resemblance at all to what I'd been saying. I couldn't believe it. Had all that chanting I'd been doing been in vain? Had my poor dog been traumatised for nothing? I couldn't help thinking that was the case. After all, if you'd been told that the secret password to an enchanted kingdom was Cabernet Sauvignon and you turned up hollering 'cabinet sew-vye-ig-non!' there's no way anyone would let you in. But this wasn't the only thing I'd been getting wrong. Rather than gently uttering the words in a softly lilting sing-song voice the way I'd been doing, it turned out that followers of Nichiren prefer to yell – or at least, that's how it seemed to my untrained ears, as the group's participants set about chanting at the tops of their voices, and at about one hundred miles per hour. There was no melody to their chanting. It was rapid fire and monotone. Another key difference was that, instead of chanting to a confused-looking dog, as I'd been doing, they chanted to a scroll housed inside a small wooden cabinet. Instead of focusing on what I wanted to achieve as I tried to chant along (quietly, oh, so quietly), I found myself obsessing over what the neighbours must be thinking at the sound of seven adults yelling the same five words in Japanese over and over again. What did they think was happening in here? Some kind of protest, with only one slogan? However, the members of the group all seemed really nice, and once the *thirty minutes*(!) of chanting were over I really enjoyed chatting to them. They seemed so energised by their practice and they all had incredible tales of how chanting had helped them, so I decided to stick with it for a while and see what happened.

What happened was that I found a great way of getting focused on my goals and quietening my mind, but I didn't really feel closer to the Something More I was seeking. Of course, I still didn't know exactly *what* I was seeking, I just knew that I hadn't found it. Although all of the followers of Nichiren Buddhism I met credited their practice with transforming their lives, it wasn't quite working for me. I had, however, made an important first step on my journey.

Something More

Nam-myoho-renge-kyo

If you feel you could benefit from more focus in your life, peace in your heart and clarity in your mind, try chanting 'Nam-myoho-renge-kyo'. There are loads of recordings on YouTube that will help you with pronunciation, pace and rhythm – so you don't make the same rookie error as me. I particularly like the videos by Tina Turner and Deva Premal. When you've found a recording that you like, take some time when you won't be interrupted, sit in a comfortable upright position and begin chanting along. It can help to have something to chant to, just as the followers of Nicherin chant to a scroll. You could focus on the flame of a candle or the picture of something that symbolises love or peace. I like to chant to the picture of a lotus flower, as it reminds me of the core teachings of the *Lotus Sutra* and the power of cause and effect. While you chant think of an effect that you would like to bring about. This could be some kind of personal goal, or a broader desire for love and peace. Whatever you chant for, don't get bogged down in specific details. Chant for the highest possible outcome for all concerned. Once you've finished, jot down any interesting thoughts or reflections from the experience in your journal.

Try chanting for at least five minutes every day for a week and make a note of any changes you observe, both internally and externally. Did you experience any breakthroughs? Did you have any weird moments of synchronicity? Do you feel calmer and more focused? If you're going through a difficult time, try chanting for longer than five minutes, and again, make a note of any differences this brings. You can find out more about Nicherin Buddhism at www.sgi.org.

3

WHAT WOULD JESUS DO?

Love your neighbour as yourself.

JESUS

J ust as I was realising that I still hadn't found what I was
looking for, posters started going up in the village advertising the Alpha Course. The course was run by the Christian
Church as an introduction for non-followers and the curious. I'd
recently read an article about Alpha by a journalist who'd been
very cynical about religion but who had been impressed by how
open and relaxed it had been. They don't try to brainwash you
and you have total freedom to say and ask whatever you like,
was the gist of his piece. Due to my parents' earlier hostility
towards religion, it had never even crossed my mind to attend
a church service – not even after my experience in the Great
Ormond Street Hospital chapel. But in more recent years both
of my parents had returned to faith. My mum had become a

Christian again and my dad, who'd been so angry towards the Catholic Church throughout my childhood, had started studying spiritual teachings. I'd seen the mellowing effect this was having on him and part of me was intrigued. When I saw that the Alpha Course also included a free, home-cooked meal, I was sold. *What do I have to lose?* I thought to myself as I signed up for the course. It turned out that I had nothing to lose and a lot to gain. However, as was to happen so frequently on my quest for Something More, the gains were nothing I could have ever forseen.

There were two Christian churches in the village – an Anglican High Church one and a Baptist one. A couple of weeks before the Alpha Course started I decided to give one of them a go. For the first time in my forty years on the planet, I entered the lion's den and attended a Sunday service. Going purely on aesthetics, as I had no other, deeper spiritual knowledge to base my decision on, I picked the High Church. The church itself was a beautiful medieval building, all grey stone and stained glass, filled with that musty incense fragrance unique to old churches. As I took my seat that first Sunday I felt nervous, self-conscious and very alone. No one said hello to me and as a single mum, with tattoos and piercings to boot, I felt that I stuck out like a sore thumb. Most of the parishioners were snowy-haired pensioners, and to quote the renowned spiritual guru Bridget Jones, 'smug marrieds'. For some weird reason, sitting among all these glowy faced, sensibly dressed families, I felt my single status acutely. My bare ring finger seemed to shine like a beacon. And of course it wasn't just that I was single – I was divorced. I wasn't exactly sure what the Bible had to say about divorced people, but I knew it wasn't good and probably involved sin. I could feel all of my old anti-religion hackles rising. *How dare these sensibly dressed, non-pierced people judge me? So what if I was divorced? What was their problem anyway?* Of course, no one had actually said any of these things to me – these were all my own fears and insecurities playing on a loop inside my head.

I can't remember much about the service other than the vicar sweeping down the aisle in his white and black robes, lots of readings from the Bible, which I didn't really understand, and the hymns reminding me of school. It was interesting to finally experience a church service at the ripe old age of forty, but I watched it with the detachment of an observer. I didn't feel moved in any way. I didn't feel that elusive Something More that I was seeking, and once the service was over my sense of detachment only grew. Not a single person spoke to me. I felt awkward and embarrassed, and went home unsure if Alpha was such a good idea after all. *To hell with all this God business*, I thought to myself angrily as I set up an account on the dating site eharmony, *I'm going to find me a man.* But as I prepared to enter the dating world once again, something inside me told me that I should still attend Alpha. I had a hunch I'd find something important there. It also helped that the first message I received from a guy on eharmony included the immortal line: 'How do you feel about teeth? It's just that I lost most of mine when I took a shed-load of acid in my twenties.'

So, one cold February night, I set off for my first Alpha class. The course was being held in a large function room attached to the Anglican church. Dining tables had been set up throughout the room and the serving hatches along one of the walls were crammed with trays of home-made lasagne; the air was rich with the aroma of tomatoes and oregano. There was a lot of laughter and chatter, and the whole ambience was instantly far more welcoming and warm than my Sunday church-service experience had been. Upon arriving, we were each shown to our assigned table. It turned out that we'd be staying with the same group of people for the duration of the course. Each group included two existing members of the church to answer any questions, and the others were all newbies like me. I was on a table with the minister from the Baptist church, another woman and, randomly, three guys called Andy. We made our introductions and tucked into huge portions of lasagne and garlic bread. By the time the meal was over I knew I'd made the right decision in coming – and it wasn't just because of the delicious food. I really liked the people I was sitting with and how open we were allowed to be with our doubts or cynicism.

The night began with a video from the guy in charge of Alpha, a curate at the Holy Trinity Church in Brompton, the Reverend Nicky Gumbel. In the video he began by outlining the historical evidence that Jesus did exist. Then he went on to say that there were three possible explanations for Jesus's claim to be the son of God:

1. He was insane.
2. He was a liar.
3. He was telling the truth.

I have to admit that I was pleasantly surprised at the candour; that there was an acknowledgement at least that Jesus could have been lying or deranged.

After the video finished we broke up into our groups to talk about what we'd seen and ask any questions we might have. One of the Andys at my table was pretty cynical – he'd only come along because his wife was Christian and he wanted to try and see if he could find any common ground for the sake of his marriage. The Baptist minister at our table answered his questions honestly and with humour. He even spoke about his own moments of doubt. This was an eye-opener for me. It hadn't occurred to me that members of the clergy could sometimes doubt the existence of God too – and the minister's admission about the vulnerabilities of the Christian faith made the whole thing seemed more accessible somehow. Although I can't remember much of the specific conversation we had that night, I vividly remember how it made me feel. I really enjoyed sitting there, talking to these people – people I'd probably never get to meet in my day-to-day life – about something as important as why we're all here, and who or what created all of this. It felt intimate and infinite all at the same time.

Two quotes from Jesus referred to during the evening had quite an effect on me. One was 'Love your neighbour as yourself' and the other was 'Love your enemy'. I'd heard both of them before, of course. But before I'd been so dismissive of the Christian faith that they'd always been like background noise, lumped in with all the 'thou shalt nots' from the Old Testament. But on that first night of Alpha I let the words sink in, and was really surprised at how they made me feel. Rather than being an opiate for the masses, this Jesus guy seemed to be all about love and lifting people up – even his enemies. However, as soon as I'd had this revelation I was confronted by a massive riddle: if Jesus was all about loving ourselves and our neighbours – and even our enemies – why had there been so much bloodshed in the name of Christianity? And I wasn't just thinking about the Crusades. In recent years both Tony Blair and George Bush had talked about their Christian faith in relation to waging a brutal onslaught on Iraq, in which hundreds of thousands of civilians were killed. How could they square this with the loving teachings of their religious leader? It didn't make sense. How can you worship someone who preached about the importance of loving your enemies while simultaneously bombing the hell out of them? But what did make sense to me was Jesus's message that love was the answer; that this was the only escape from the cycle of fear. His words struck me deep inside like heart-seeking missiles. And, although I still had so many questions, I did have the beginnings of an answer. I'd finally found the Something More that I felt had been missing from my Buddhist practice. I'd found spiritual love – or what the ancient Greeks called *agape*, meaning 'the highest form of love'.

The more I thought about love as a spiritual thing (rather than an emotional or romantic one), the more I was struck by the revolutionary aspects of Jesus's teachings. All week after that first Alpha meeting I pondered the concepts that had burrowed themselves deep inside me. Previously, I'd always thought 'love your neighbour as yourself' meant being a good person to others. But now the two words 'as yourself' kept jumping out at me. Why had Jesus said that? Why hadn't he just said 'love your neighbour'?

At the next Alpha meeting I brought this up over our meal. It was clear that no one else at the table had really paid much attention to the 'as yourself' before either. I asked the group members if they thought Jesus was saying that it was essential that we loved ourselves in order to be able to love another? The Andys seemed a little nonplussed about this, to be honest, but as a life coach I'd read various self-help books about self-love. One of them had even convinced me to write 'Hello, beautiful' in lipstick on my bathroom mirror, to remind me to be nice to my reflection. You can imagine how this went down with my teenage son. But naff affirmations aside, I was already familiar with the concept of self-love. I'd always assumed it to be an export from California; a product of the green-juice-quaffing self-help brigade. But here was Jesus some two thousand plus years before, preaching the same gospel. Once again, my 'opiate of the masses' beliefs about Christianity were being challenged. As far as I could see there was nothing oppressive about telling people that they ought to love themselves – quite the opposite, in fact. Why, then, was Christianity – and most particularly the Catholic Church – so obsessed with guilt and sin? I was confused but also intrigued.

So the following Sunday, I decided to give the Baptist church a go. It had snowed in the night and the village looked magical in the winter sunlight, with the snow-covered streets and trees glimmering white-gold. I took the short walk bundled up in my coat and wellies feeling nervous but hopeful. The Baptist minister had been so friendly and approachable at Alpha, and hopefully his church would be too.

It couldn't have been more different from my experience at the Anglican church. The minute I walked in, stamping the snow from my boots, I was warmly welcomed by two meeters and greeters. As soon as I took a seat the person next to me immediately introduced themselves and we had a lovely chat. Then the music began. This time there was no choir, no sweeping pomp and ceremony. The minister took to the floor dressed in jeans and a jumper and introduced the church band. There was a drummer, a bassist and two guitarists. Of course, the songs they were performing were Christian songs, but I found the whole rock vibe far more engaging. I clearly wasn't alone. The music seemed to work its way inside everyone, energising the entire room. People were swaying, tapping and nodding along. Some even had their hands in the air – a massive deal in buttoned-up Britain. When the band began playing 'Amazing Grace', the weirdest thing happened – my eyes filled with tears. I had no idea why, other than that it sounded like the sweetest, saddest thing I'd ever heard. I felt uplifted, moved and most of all, connected. I wasn't exactly sure what I was connected *to*. I just had the feeling that I'd been plugged into something far bigger than myself, like a wave suddenly aware that it belongs to an entire ocean. In Arabic culture, and particularly within Sufism, a mystical branch of Islam, a transcendental experience induced by music like this is known as *tarab* and is actively practised as a way of connecting to the divine. I gazed up at the plain wooden cross hanging on the wall behind the band and found myself asking: *Are you there, God? Are you real?*

As with the music, the sermon was very different from the one given at the Anglican church. There were Bible readings, but this time they were part of a much wider talk. The minister spoke about 'resting in God's love'. This was an idea that really appealed to me. Previously I'd been under the apprehension that religion required a lot of work: so much striving to be good; so much guilt for being a sinner; so many commandments; so many opportunities to fall short of. But simply resting in love felt beautiful in its simplicity. I stored away the notion in my heart, next to loving my neighbour, myself and my enemy.

After the sermon there were prayers, but instead of it just being the minister who prayed, anyone was able to pray out loud if they felt called to do so. There were also periods of silence for private prayer and contemplation. The whole thing felt really organic and very inclusive. And then, to finish, there was another rousing round of songs. After the service was over people congregated in the room at the back for coffee and tea. Once again, I was welcomed into conversations and I walked home through the snow bubbling with joy. Had I finally found what I was looking for? The sense of connection I felt that morning certainly felt like Something More.

In the days following the Baptist church service, I decided to try and start putting what I'd learnt into practice. I'd sit in meditation and try to rest in Love (still uncomfortable with the concept of God and all of the negative connotations that entailed for me, I decided to refer to God as Love with a capital L instead; it felt simpler that way, cleaner). I took great solace from the notion of 'resting in Love' because the assumption is that the Love is there already; there's no need to seek or find, you simply have to rest and allow it to be. On some days my Resting in Love meditations worked a lot better than on others. Often, Resting in Love was ambushed by its nemesis, Wrestling With To Do Lists, and my mind would fill with inane chatter about what to buy for dinner and whether or not I should polish the skirting boards. But every so often, I'd manage to fully let go and I'd feel a weightless sensation akin to floating on my back in the sea. It was a beautiful feeling and once again it left me feeling connected to something far greater than me; a gentle yet powerful force.

Something More

Self-love inventory

How loving are you towards yourself? For the next week make a conscious effort to monitor your self-talk. When you catch your inner voice saying something negative, ask yourself if this is how you would talk to a friend. We get so used to our inner voice and its constant commentary that we can lose sight of how negative or harsh it can be. In your journal, write a list of some of your most commonly used self-criticisms. These could be things like: 'I'm not attractive enough,' 'I'm so stupid,' or 'There's no way I'll get the job.' Then write alternative, loving statements for each of them – the kind of things you would say to a friend. For example: 'I'm beautiful inside and out,' 'I'm wise and intelligent,' 'I have everything I need to get the job.'

In what other ways could you be more loving towards yourself? Write three ideas in your journal – and do each of them in the coming week.

Resting in Love meditation

Find some time when you won't be interrupted and put your phone on silent, if you are using one. Sit or lie in a comfortable position. and take a few deep and calming breaths. Working up from your feet, breathe into every part of your body until you're fully relaxed. Then visualise yourself floating on your back in a warm, golden sea. Feel all the tension being drained from you and drifting off in the water. Picture yourself being bathed in golden love. Feel that love soaking into every cell of your body, from the top of your head to the tips of your toes, until you feel as if you've become one with an ocean of peace. If it helps, repeat the mantra 'resting in love' over and over, out loud or silently. If any thoughts pop up – and they will – picture them floating high above you like clouds in the sky, completely separate from you. Watch them with the detached air of an observer as they disappear from view. With every out-breath feel yourself sinking deeper and deeper into a sea of love.

Start making the Resting in Love meditation part of your daily routine. Write about how it makes you feel in your journal. If you like meditating to music, 'In the Stillness' by Karen Drucker is a great soundtrack for this meditation. You can find it on YouTube.

4

THE POWER OF PRAYER

When I pray coincidences happen,
and when I don't, they don't.

WILLIAM TEMPLE

When I was a child a singer called Paul Young had a hit with a song called 'Every Time You Go Away'. 'Every time you go away you take a piece of me with you,' the chorus went. Only that's not how I heard it. I thought he was singing 'Every time you go away you take a piece of *meat* with you,' so I imagined Paul Young's lover leaving him brandishing a sausage or a pork chop. I had a similar confusion with the first prayer I was ever taught – the Lord's Prayer – which we had to recite every day in school assembly.

Lord's Prayer

Our Father who art in heaven
Hallowed be thy name.
Thy kingdom come
Thy will be done,
On earth as it is in heaven.
Give us this day our daily bread
And forgive us our trespasses,
As we forgive those who trespass against us.
And lead us not into temptation,
But deliver us from evil.
For thine is the kingdom,
The power and the glory.
Forever and ever, amen.

From the age of five until about seven I merrily chanted, 'Are father, who art in heaven, Harold be thy name.' I didn't stop to question the fact that this really didn't make any sense because none of the Lord's Prayer made any sense to me. I had no idea what 'Thy kingdom come' meant and I didn't get why we had to ask to be given our 'daily bread' but not our daily cake, sweets or biscuits. And how were we supposed to be 'delivered' from evil? By the postman, like parcels? We were never told in assembly *why* we had to say the Lord's Prayer. It was just something we did on auto-pilot as part of the daily routine, like putting our chairs on the tops of the tables at the end of the day. So when I started going to the Baptist church, I was shocked to discover that I still knew all the words of the Lord's Prayer off by heart, despite not having uttered them for almost thirty years (I have the same uncanny ability when it comes to Johnny Cash's song lyrics, thanks to my dad). But this time I was determined not to just recite the words of the prayer, parrot-fashion; I wanted context, and meaning.

The Lord's Prayer appears in the Bible as part of Jesus's famous Sermon on the Mount. In his book *The Gospel According to Jesus*, Stephen Mitchell breaks down the Lord's Prayer for a modern-day readership. When Jesus says, 'Thy kingdom come,' Mitchell says he is talking about finding 'heaven' (or Love) in the here and now, within ourselves. And it turns out that when Jesus said 'Give us this day our daily bread,' he wasn't talking about a nice sliced loaf, but about daily spiritual nourishment. Regarding the final part of the prayer, which had always stumped me as a child: 'But deliver us from evil,' Mitchell argues that Jesus is asking for us to be spared from pain.

Despite having a better grasp of the Lord's Prayer I still felt very self-conscious about praying, and as a woman, I felt a real resistance to praying to a male God constantly personified as a 'Lord' or 'Father'. Then two things happened that were nothing short of miracles – or coincidences, depending on your level of cynicism. Since my introduction to Christianity I'd been conveniently avoiding the trickiest of Jesus's teachings – that of loving your enemy. To be fair, I didn't exactly have any enemies as such, but I did have a couple of problematic relationships in my life. One of these relationships was with a long-term friend who had a habit of lapsing into passive-aggressive mode the minute she was under pressure. When things were going well, she was all sweetness and light, an absolute joy to be around, but when things were going badly she could fire off a back-handed compliment or a snarky dig quicker than you could say 'ouch!' Past classics included: 'Wow, you're so brave wearing that!' and 'You've got a book deal with Hodder & Stoughton? But they're a proper publisher.' Never has the humble word 'but' been so loaded.

When I first started giving the concept of loving your enemy some serious thought my relationship with my friend was fraught. I'd had just about enough. Yes, I understood that she was going through a tough time – her marriage was permanently on the rocks and her job was stressful – but I was fed up with being her emotional punchbag. I'd started to distance myself from her and even just thinking about her made me prickle with indignation. So, when I searched my life for an enemy to practise loving on, she immediately sprang to mind – but how could I love her without getting hurt, or giving myself a tension headache from the pent-up desire to kick her in the leg? This thought was preying on my mind one day when I was killing some time in the local library. As I browsed the shelves I came across a book called *Life's Little Detours* by Regina Brett. I randomly flicked to a page and immediately saw the words: 'If you have a resentment you want to be free of . . .' Well, yes, I did, so I read on.

The words turned out to be part of a quote from an article by a Christian minister, and he went on to advise that if you resent a person you should pray for them, and not only pray for them but pray that they receive everything you would want for yourself – a kind of mash-up of the two Jesus quotes: 'Love your enemy as yourself.' I thought about praying for my passive-aggressive friend, the person who had hurt me so deeply over the years, and praying for all the things I would want for myself – and it made me feel physically sick. She doesn't deserve it, was my first thought. But according to the minister quoted in Brett's book, even if you don't really mean it you should pray anyway, and after two weeks of daily praying you'll apparently find that you've actually come to mean the words. Hmm. I wasn't at all convinced, but I jotted down the idea and ordered a copy of Brett's book anyway.

That night, after my Resting in Love meditation, which was only slightly ruined by the sound of my dog Max chomping on a bone, I attempted to pray for my passive-aggressive friend. First, of course, I had to make a mental list of everything I would pray for for myself. Happiness, career success and romantic love – they all seemed so nice when I thought of them in the context of me. However, when I thought of them in the context of my so-called friend they made me seethe. Why should I wish happiness on someone who'd caused me so much pain? There was especially no way I wanted to wish her romantic love – not when my own romantic disasters had clearly caused her so much pleasure in the past. Nonetheless, I went through the motions and prayed through some seriously gritted teeth. This was going to be a fun couple of weeks. Thank you, Jesus.

On the second night it was more of the same, but by the third, something weird happened. As I prayed for my friend to find love, I thought of her husband's repeated infidelities and how deeply unhappy they must have made her. I thought of the pain she must have felt with every fresh gut-wrenching discovery, and of the fear that was keeping her trapped in a loveless marriage. This was something I could personally relate to. No wonder my friend lashed out sometimes – she was deeply unhappy. This time, when I prayed for her to find love, I genuinely meant it. She deserved to be happy. We all do. As my mindset shifted I felt a softening in my heart too. It felt good to love someone who had caused me pain. Rather than feeling stupid for doing so, or weak, I felt incredibly strong, and once again connected to a source of strength far greater than me.

This would have been enough of a miracle in itself, but a week later something even stranger happened. My friend called to say she'd be passing close to my nearest town on her way home from a conference and asked if I fancied meeting for a coffee. If this had happened a couple of weeks earlier I'd probably have made an excuse and declined, but having been praying for her happiness for the past few days, and softening in my feelings towards her, I readily agreed. We met up for coffee and it was so much fun and easy-going that the coffee turned into lunch. We ended up spending about three hours together without a moment of awkwardness or the hint of a barbed remark. Then, when I walked her back to her car, she turned to me and said, completely out of the blue, 'I just want to say sorry.' Taken aback, I asked her what for. 'For the times in the past when I've been a real bitch to you,' she replied. She then went on to mention a couple of specific incidents and give me a detailed explanation as to why she'd said what she had. The crux of the matter was that she was deeply unhappy, and sometimes seeing my life situation and feeling envious of it made her feel worse. 'I'm truly sorry,' she finished, with tears in her eyes. As I hugged her I started crying too. 'It's so weird,' she said through her tears. 'I hadn't planned to say any of that to you – I just felt this sudden urge to.'

After we'd said goodbye and I walked away I couldn't help wondering whether this was evidence of the transformative power of loving your enemy, even if the love you show them isn't directly to their face. Could they somehow pick up on the love you direct their way through thoughts and prayers, and respond in kind? Of course, it all could have been a coincidence, but the tingling I felt running up and down my spine made me hope that it wasn't – that it was indeed proof of the power of Love.

The following Sunday I went to the evening service at the Baptist church. The evening service was more low key than the morning one – there were fewer people and no children so it was a lot quieter. But in some ways this made it all the more powerful. There was an intimacy and softness to it, kind of like an 'unplugged' gig. We began the evening by praying. I was way too self-conscious to pray out loud like some people were doing, so I closed my eyes and focused on feeling Love instead. I'm not sure if it was the collective energy in the room or the soothing soundtrack of others praying in the background, but this time I felt more connected to Something More than ever before. And I overflowed with gratitude. All I wanted to do was say thank you – not out loud, of course, but inside my head I gave thanks over and over again. I gave thanks for my son, our home, our new life in the beautiful countryside, the amazing opportunities I'd been given as a writer and the book I was about to have published. I was awash with thanks.

Then the minister asked us to move our chairs to the side of the room and asked a couple of guys to help him fetch a huge map of the world from the back of the church. They laid the map down on the floor in the centre of the church and we all gathered round. The minister lit a tea-light and placed it on the UK.

'I feel that we're being called to pray for the rest of the world,' he explained. 'The flame of the candle represents the power of our prayer. If you feel called to pray for another country or someone in that country, please do.'

We closed our eyes and one by one, people began offering prayers – for war-torn countries, for oppressed populations, for friends and family members overseas. At one point I opened my eyes and gazed at the map. Once again I felt connected to something far greater than myself, something that covered the entire world. When the praying had come to a natural conclusion the minister blew out the candle and we went back to our seats. Walking home later beneath an inky-black sky I saw how praying for others and sending out thoughts of love could light up the world, just like the stars lit up the night sky above me.

A couple of weeks later the second prayer-based miracle/ coincidence happened. I'd recently started running a writing course for a charity called Centrepoint. It is based in London and offers hostel accommodation and other support for teenagers who have been made homeless. I'd wanted to offer the course as a way of giving the participants an opportunity to channel the traumatic experiences they'd been through into pieces of writing. It hadn't been going as well as I'd hoped. At the first session only a handful of girls turned up. It turned out that most of them were caught up in a drama involving a boy at the hostel and preferred to talk about how some boys should be neutered 'like they do to dogs'. The only girl who wasn't caught up in the drama sat in silence throughout the session, a woolly hat pulled down low over her face.

It was exactly the same the following week and it was hard not to feel disheartened. My head started filling with doubts. Maybe I wasn't cut out for this kind of work. Maybe I wasn't able to help after all. Yes, I'd grown up on a pretty rough council estate and witnessed crime and poverty at first hand, but I'd never been homeless. These teenagers probably saw me as a middle-class do-gooder who had no idea what they were going through. But there was something about the silent girl in the woolly hat that intrigued me. Even though she never said anything she was the only one who seemed to be listening to what I had to say.

So, on the day of my third session at the charity, I decided to put the power of prayer to the test again and went to the morning prayer meeting at church. And when I say morning, I mean *extreme morning*, for the meetings began at 6 a.m. Due to the ungodly hour only about ten people turned up, but I found it extremely powerful nonetheless. We all sat in a circle and one of the guys played his guitar softly into silence. Then, if we felt called to, we could say a prayer out loud. For the first time, I found the confidence to speak. I still didn't feel comfortable with all the 'Lords' and 'Fathers' the others used in their prayers, so I kept it as simple as possible. 'Please could you guide me to say the right thing in my workshop at Centrepoint today. Please could you help me connect with the girl who doesn't say anything. Please help me to help her.' I sat in silence once again, then, to my delight and surprise, various members of the group started praying for me and the girl too. Just as on the night we all prayed for the world, I felt plugged into a powerful network of hope and love.

That evening, a miracle happened. At first it appeared to be a disaster. I've since learnt that this is often the way with miracles – they often come disguised as catastrophes. Only one person turned up to my workshop – the girl who never said anything. I asked her if she'd still like me to go ahead with the class and she nodded. I said a quick silent prayer, just to remind anyone or anything that might be listening that I really, really needed their help, then I began. The exercise I had planned was a guided visualisation where I get people to close their eyes and picture the main character from their story arriving back home. It was an exercise I'd done many times in writing workshops and I knew the script off by heart. I asked the girl to close her eyes and picture her main character, then talked her through the scenario. 'See your character walking down the street where they live. What do they see? Smell? Hear? Now picture them arriving at their home, walking up to their front door. As they open the door what do they see, smell, hear? Is there anyone else at home …' And so it went on as I got the girl to picture her character going into each of the rooms in the house until finally reaching their bedroom. I stuck to the usual script, asking her to picture the bedroom. Was it tidy or messy? What was in the cupboards? What was on the walls? Then, just as I was about to finish, a completely unscripted question popped from my mouth: 'Your character spots something on the bed – what is it?'

Then I got the girl to open her eyes and write down any useful details she'd gleaned from the exercise. To my relief she started writing away furiously. Once she'd finished I decided to take a risk and ask her to talk me through her notes. She began to talk – and talk and talk. She told me about how her story was based around the London estate she grew up on – an estate ruled by gangs, where simply wandering into the wrong postcode could get you beaten up or worse. Her main character was a teenage boy who'd been tempted into a life of crime as a gang member. She told me how she'd imagined his home to be, and how she'd pictured him coming back home to get ready to commit a crime. 'But then something weird happened,' she said. 'When you asked me what he saw on his bed I saw a Bible. It's really strange,' she continued, 'because I hadn't seen him as being religious before.'

I somehow managed to play it cool and asked her how she thought the appearance of a Bible could add to her story.

'It could make him more sympathetic,' she replied, 'if I show him torn between his faith and the gang. It could give the story more hope too – if he ends up choosing his faith and turning his back on crime.'

I felt a shiver course through my body. What had just happened? Had our morning prayers sparked a chain reaction that resulted in God popping up unexpectedly in this girl's story? My brain said it had to be a coincidence, but my heart was beating so fast it was as if it knew something else to be true.

On my way home that night I rang my dad excitedly and told him what had happened. 'It has to be a coincidence, right?' I asked. He laughed and shared a quote with me from a former Archbishop of Canterbury named William Temple: 'When I pray, coincidences happen, and when I don't, they don't.' I took this to be the perfect answer. After all, it didn't really matter how it had happened – what mattered was that it *had* happened. One way or another, my prayer had been answered.

For the rest of my course with Centrepoint the no-longer-silent girl was the only person who turned up. I mentored her with her writing, then, once the course had finished, I managed to get her a work-experience placement at the publishing company I was freelancing for. Ordinarily the young people we'd get there on work experience would be the upper class offspring of friends of the bosses. They'd show up late, sit at their computers looking bored, then return to their private schools, work-experience box ticked. Seeing my girl turning up on time, working her butt off every day and drinking in every last drop of the opportunity she was being given was one of the most rewarding experiences of my writing career.

Subsequently, praying has become one of my most powerful spiritual tools. Here's what I've learnt so far about how prayer should be: it should be messy, free-flowing, rough around the edges and full to the brim with heart – *your* heart. Prayer is where we connect to Love. It's where we give thanks and ask for help and express wonder. And remember to listen. That part is really important. When I first started a regular practice of praying I was all about the talking. I'd whisper or speak out loud great monologues about what was going on in my life, what was troubling me and where I needed guidance. I'd finish with a request for strength or love or peace, then I'd be up and off on my merry way. It was the Baptist minister who first introduced the notion of prayer to me as a *two-way* conversation. 'You have to give God the chance to reply,' he said. 'And you have to listen for his reply.'

So I adapted my prayer practice slightly. Now, as well as talking, I spend even more time listening. I've learnt that love doesn't always answer immediately. Sometimes it does. At times I'll pose a question that's been really troubling me, and almost instantly I hear an inner voice of wisdom provide me with the breakthrough I've been craving. But often I'll pray and sit in silence, waiting and listening, and no answer comes. So, I'll get on with my day, but with an attitude of openness and expectation – my eyes open wide for any sign of guidance, however it might come. And it always does come – in the shape of a chance meeting, a random sign, a bizarre coincidence or serendipity.

The more practice you put into prayer, the stronger your connection with Love will be – and the more intrinsic it will become to your daily routine. You'll find yourself praying anywhere and everywhere – at the bus stop, in a meeting, on a date or in the queue to pay for your shopping. And you'll realise that Love isn't only accessible via a priest or religious pomp and ceremony. Love is accessible everywhere. Love wants to hear from you anytime. It's waiting and wanting to guide you home.

Something More

Four prayers

I'd like to share four of my favourite prayers with you - prayers that have really helped me over the past few years. If you feel resistance to praying to a god, take some time to work out who or what you would feel comfortable praying to, for example the Universe, the Creative Source, your inner wisdom or simply Love.

> **Praying for your enemy** Is there someone in your life that you have a difficult relationship with? Maybe not an 'enemy' as such, but someone who has hurt or angered you in some way. Today, pray for that person that they will receive everything you would wish for yourself. Pray through gritted teeth if need be - just do whatever it takes. Do the same thing again tomorrow and for the next couple of weeks. Write about how this makes you feel in your journal. Notice any change in your feelings towards this person - and any subsequent changes in your relationship.
>
> *Ho'oponopono* The Hawaiians have a prayer called *Ho'oponopono*, which is a prayer for reconciliation and forgiveness. I love it for its simplicity. All you have to do is repeat the following mantra over and over: 'I'm sorry, please forgive me, thank you, I love you.'

As you repeat the prayer, think about someone you've hurt or let down in some way. Then pray it for someone you need to forgive. Picture telling them that you're sorry and asking for their forgiveness. Then thank them and tell them that you love them. How does it feel? Really hard at first, I bet. But stick with it, because it's so healing. Often, when we're angry with another we get stuck in our own victimhood – I know I do. The other person becomes the source of all wrong-doing and you feel smug in your self-righteousness. But this comes at a price – you stay stuck in your anger and bitterness too. Practise *Ho'oponopono* to help release yourself from anger and resentment. Keep saying the prayer about the person you need to forgive – until you find a reason to actually mean it.

The Serenity Prayer The Serenity Prayer was written by American theologian Reinhold Niebuhr in the 1930s, and was later adopted by Alcoholics Anonymous and used in their twelve-step programme. It has appeared in several forms, the best known of which is this:

> God, grant me the serenity to accept the
>   things I cannot change,
> Courage to change the things I can,
> And the Wisdom to know the difference.

I love this version of the Serenity Prayer because it says so much in so few words about how to successfully negotiate our way through life. So often, we try to have power over things that are way out of our control. We try to manipulate outcomes and make people change, with frustrating and sometimes devastating consequences. Equally, in situations where things are within our control, we can allow fear to hold us back, later to become plagued by 'if onlys'. We need courage in these situations to make the changes required. And we need the wisdom to be able to differentiate between the times when we need to step up and the times when we need to let go. Saying the Serenity Prayer daily is a great way of reminding ourselves that we can't control everything.

What would you have me do? Early into my exploration of Christianity, I came across a book called *A Course in Miracles* by Helen Schucman. The book is full of daily lessons, including this daily prayer, which encourages you to hand yourself over to the guidance of Something More, expanding on the concept of 'Thy will be done'. *A Course in Miracles* recommends saying the prayer every morning before starting your day:

Where would You have me go?
What would You have me do?
What would You have me say?
And to whom?

I have a copy of the prayer on my bedroom wall. When I say the prayer, I picture the 'You' referred to as Love. I love the way it helps me hand over my day to Love before it's even begun. I love the notion of making myself a channel for Love in all of my adventures and my interactions with others. Obviously, I don't always remember the intention of the prayer once I'm going about my day. Some days I forget it altogether and spiral down into distraction or fear, but by saying the prayer on a regular basis, I'm getting a whole lot better at putting Love at the heart of my life and letting it guide me. In the words of Rabbi Abraham Joshua Heschel, 'It is precisely the function of prayer to shift the centre of living from self-consciousness to self-surrender.' By praying daily we help surrender our ego to Love and away from fear.

Create a prayer box

It can really help to write down your more personal prayers, either in your journal or on scraps of paper that you could then place in a jar or box. Not only does the act of writing make your prayers seem more concrete somehow, but it can also be interesting to look back at them, using the benefit of hindsight to see how they were answered – often in ways you would never have imagined.

5

SAINTLY SEXISM

Wives, be subject to your husbands as though to
the Lord, for the man is the head of the woman.

ST PAUL

As I continued to explore Christianity through the Alpha course I felt increasingly torn. I loved the Love at the heart of Jesus's teachings and the way it was transforming me and my life, but I hated the fear I found in so many of the other practices and doctrines. There appeared to be fear of other faiths, fear of sex, fear of women – for how else would you explain the need to judge and oppress huge swathes of society based solely on their spiritual choices, gender or sexuality? One night I stomped home from church in a rage, after a sermon condemning sex outside of marriage for being a sin. I couldn't believe that I – and millions of other people like me, who for whatever reason had chosen not to marry – was being judged like this. How dare the Church condemn people for not marrying? How dare it tell people what they could and couldn't do with their bodies? I was so angry that I slept with a detective I'd just started dating. (Note: it turns out that 'I'll show you shags' aren't always that spiritually empowering, especially if the person you sleep with turns out to be obsessed with sports cars and the sizes of their engines.) But I digress. I was so angry and hurt by the sermon that I stopped going to church for a couple of weeks. But then I really missed the teachings about Love and the powerful prayer experiences. I felt an emptiness opening up inside me, so I decided to give the Church one last chance.

Towards the end of the Alpha course you go on a retreat. The idea behind the retreat is to give participants the chance to fully immerse themselves in all they've learnt and the opportunity to become a Christian. Our retreat was a day spent in a beautiful old church in a nearby village. The night before I wrote in my diary: 'I have a feeling I will finally reach the crossroads tomorrow and make my choice. And I have a feeling I know exactly what I will choose.' I was convinced I'd end up overcoming my doubts and joining the Church, but when I got home the following evening I wrote: 'Back from the Alpha day and feeling really confused. I thought I'd feel elated and full of joy but I actually feel really sad and lonely.'

It couldn't have been a more beautiful day for our retreat. It was the first properly warm day of spring, the sky was cornflower blue and the church grounds were bursting with bright clusters of daffodils. We went into the church and watched two films about the Holy Spirit. As I sat there in the darkness on the old wooden pew I got more and more nervous. Becoming a Christian felt like such a huge commitment. Forget about the

Holy Spirit – the free spirit in me felt cornered and ready to flee. I also felt incredibly lonely all of a sudden, and ambushed by old fears. My life felt littered with mistakes and bad decisions, and I was overwhelmed with regret. At the end of the day we were given the opportunity to receive prayer. I took it. I needed it. I needed something to stop my slide into despair. The Baptist minister and a guy from the other church both placed their hands on my shoulders and prayed for me. Tears slid down my face. I didn't know what to do. The moment of clarity I'd been hoping for didn't come. I felt worse than I'd done in a long time.

When I got home the floodgates opened. I ended up curled on my bedroom floor, crying and crying. It was as if a huge ball of sorrow that had been trapped inside me for a lifetime had finally dislodged and was working its way out. I cried for my childhood self, for all of the pain and fear I'd experienced. I cried for my teenage self, for all of the loneliness and despair I'd felt. I cried for my twenty-something self and the poor decisions I'd made due to my lack of self-love. But instead of getting better it just got worse. The sorrow was engulfing me, choking me. I couldn't see even the faintest glimmer of hope. In the end I became so desperate that I prayed – a snotty, tear-streaked, gasping-for-air prayer – that if there really was a God, I would be given some kind of sign because I needed reassurance like never before. My eyes were immediately drawn to a book that had slipped beneath my bookshelf – it was only visible due to my prone position on the floor. It was a book my mum had bought me called *Finding Sanctuary* by Abbot Christopher Jamison. As I opened it a bookmark fell out. On the bookmark was printed Psalm 23.

Psalm 23

The Lord is my shepherd, I shall not want.
He makes me lie down in green pastures,
He leads me beside quiet waters,
He restores my soul.
He guides me in paths of righteousness
For his name's sake.
Even though I walk through the valley of the
    shadow of death,
I will fear no evil,
For you are with me;
Your rod and your staff,
They comfort me.
You prepare a table before me
In the presence of my enemies.
You anoint my head with oil,
My cup overflows.
Surely goodness and love will follow me
All the days of my life,
And I will dwell in the house of the Lord forever.

I studied the words and drank in the comfort they gave me. The idea of lying down in green pastures, beside quiet waters, was a balm to my aching soul. Lying there on the floor in despair felt pretty much like languishing in the valley of death, but the notion of a loving presence who was there to protect me, to shepherd me to safety, was overwhelmingly comforting, as was the line: 'Surely goodness and love will follow me all the days of my life.' I sat up straight and wiped the tears from my eyes. Then I had an epiphany. The overwhelming sorrow I'd been feeling was for what might have been, if I'd only found the path to Love sooner, if only I'd had the strength of a spiritual faith to draw upon. I was crying for all the joy I'd missed out on; for the healthy relationships I could have had, if I'd only been able to love myself enough to realise that's what I deserved. My heart ached for what could have been, but Psalm 23 made me see what *still could be* – and finally I felt hope.

The next day, I went to the morning service at church. The minister began by saying that one of the church members had died during the week and his family had requested that we sing Psalm 23. It was the first time I'd ever heard it sung there, and I couldn't help feeling a shiver at the coincidence. Our rendition of the psalm was so beautiful that when it ended the minister asked that we sing it again – another first. Then he went on to preach about the message in Psalm 23. I'd asked for a sign and now I was being given it, again and again – that, with Love as my guide, with Love to rest in, I had nothing to fear and a life overflowing with goodness to look forward to. When the service ended I sought out the minister and told him that I was ready to become a Christian.

Then the pendulum swung back again. Over the next few weeks I had many moments of doubt about becoming a Christian, mainly centred around the overwhelmingly masculine nature of the Church. All of the people quoted from the Bible in sermons were men. The minister was a man, as were the other Church leaders. God was a man – or at least portrayed that way through the language of the 'Father', the 'Son' and the 'Lord'. I wondered where the role models for the girls in the congregation were. What kind of damage was this doing to their spiritual psyches, constantly being sidelined simply because they were women? The more I read about Jesus, the more it struck me that he didn't seem to have nearly as much of an issue with women as modern-day Christians did. He travelled with women at a time and in a society where it was revolutionary to do so. Many of his parables were about women and clearly aimed at women, and his ministry was funded by women, including the infamous Mary Magdalene who, it turned out, had never been a prostitute. A pope named Gregory decided to label her as such more than five hundred years after Jesus's death, when the notion of the repentant sinner had come to form an integral part of the Church. The more I researched the teachings of Christ and early Christianity, the more shocked I became at the huge discrepancies between them and what Christianity came to be. I became adept at filtering out the things I saw as being agenda laden, and focused on the Love at the heart of Jesus's teachings instead. My dad and I started having fantastic talks about spirituality over our regular pub lunches of fish and chips. One day he gave me a card with this quote from St Paul:

If I speak in tongues of men or angels, but do not have love, I am a clanging cymbal. If I can fathom all mysteries and all knowledge, but do not have love, I am nothing. Love is patient and kind. It is not easily angered. It keeps no record of wrongs. Love always protects, trusts, hopes and perseveres. Love never fails.

This was the kind of Bible quote I could really draw inspiration from, full of simple, powerful, unconditional Love, with no judgement based on gender or sexuality – with no judgement, full stop. My lunches with my dad helped solidify my growing belief that there was only one source of spiritual Love – one God if you want to call it that – but over the millennia, humans had created their own ways of accessing and explaining this Love through different faiths and religions. I'd never really been comfortable with the whole 'our God is the one true God' notion, wherever it came from. Now I saw religions as many different routes to the same destination – and it was the destination that mattered. Moreover, it was a destination that could be reached by atheists too, because it was all about *feeling* and *experience* rather than dogma. When I went to church one Sunday and sat in the silence of prayer, the words 'go lightly' echoed through my head. I felt the presence of Something More telling me that I needed to go lightly with my faith – not get tangled up in theories and rhetoric, or get stuck in fearful thoughts inside my head, but to keep coming back into my heart and the wordless place of unconditional love I found there.

I started praying and meditating regularly – in the silence and stillness of meditation I was able to tap into a place of Love and an inner wisdom that would answer my prayers. Slowly but surely, I was creating my own personal spiritual practice with Christianity at the heart of it. I decided to book a date for my baptism. When I did so, I instantly had a test of my faith that shook me to the core. I'd just signed up for a course the church was running about putting your faith into practice. On the first night of the course about twenty of us met and sat in a large circle in a room at the back of the church. The first thing we had to do was complete a questionnaire to ascertain how well we were doing 'walking the walk' of our Christian faith. About halfway through I came across a question that really bewildered me. It went something like this: 'Men, how well do you think you're doing as the leader of your family?'

'Why does this question only refer to men?' I asked.

'Because in the Christian faith men are the leaders of their families,' a man sitting next to me replied.

'Seriously?!' I looked around the circle for some moral support. Surely the others didn't agree with this out-of-date misogyny. But no support was forthcoming. Even the other women looked away awkwardly, refusing to make eye contact.

'But that's insane,' I spluttered. 'Why can't men and women be equal partners within a marriage?'

'Because someone needs to be the head of the family,' the man's wife replied.

'Men need to be dominant within a marriage. It says so in the Bible,' the man continued. 'The trouble with the world today is there's too many strong women.' He spat out the words 'strong women' as if he was spitting out worms.

My heart began hammering in my ribcage. This was nuts. As far as I could see there was very little difference between dominant and abusive, and the thought that this was something the Bible could be seen as endorsing made my blood run cold. 'Well, then I seriously need to think twice about getting baptised,' I snapped. 'I had no idea this was what I was signing up for.'

The rest of the meeting passed by under a cloud of awkwardness, with me constantly fighting the urge to get up and leave. When it finally came to an end the minister asked if he could meet me the following day to talk about what had happened. He wanted the chance to properly explain the part of the Bible referred to. I grudgingly agreed. As I started walking home a couple of women from the meeting ran after me and told me that they didn't subscribe to the whole men being leaders of the family thing either. It was interesting and depressing to me that they hadn't said a word in my defence during the meeting, and that they clearly felt the need to keep their views secret.

The next day I met with the minister and he tried to reassure me that although it said in the Bible that wives should 'submit' to their husbands, it also instructed husbands to love their wives 'just as Christ loved the Church' (Ephesians 5:22–25). He talked about how he believed that Christian men should make the key decisions in their households but, if they truly loved their wives the way Christ loved the Church, they'd never make a decision that would hurt them. So Christian marriage was a benevolent dictatorship then. How comforting. I came away feeling confused and downhearted. How could people still subscribe to this nonsense in the twenty-first century? How could Christian men who loved and respected their wives seriously expect them to submit to their will? It was like the 'no sex outside of marriage' thing all over again. And to make matters worse, my baptism was looming. Once again, I felt utterly torn between the love I felt for 'God' as I understood God to be, that is, spiritual Love, and the hatred I felt for the archaic, misogynistic parts of the Church. Worse was to come when I found this gem from St Paul:

> And in all congregations of God's people women should keep silent at the meeting. They have no permission to talk but should keep their place as the law directs. If there is something they want to know they can ask their husbands at home. It is a shocking thing for a woman to talk at a meeting.

'What if they don't have a husband?' I raged when I read this. Who did St Paul think he was, preaching this kind of nonsense? Jesus never said anything about women not being allowed to speak. Some internet sleuthing led to the discovery that, until the New Testament was put together by a council of men in

Rome – some three hundred years after Jesus's death – women had played a very active role in the early Church. Lydia of Philippi, Phoebe, Prisca, Chloe and Junia were all women mentioned in the Letters of St Paul as having prominent roles in it. Lydia hosted church meetings in her home. Prisca was a missionary partner of Paul's. Phoebe is referred to by Paul as a deacon and Junia as an apostle. So why did Paul forbid women to speak in church when so many women were actively supporting him in his ministry? They wouldn't have been able to support him if they hadn't been allowed to speak in public. It didn't make any sense, especially when you compare it to what Paul wrote in Galations 3:28.

> So in Christ Jesus you are all children of God through faith, for all of you who were baptised into Christ have clothed yourselves with Christ. There is neither Jew nor Gentile, neither slave nor free, *nor is there male and female, for you are all one in Christ Jesus.*

Then I internet sleuthed upon a whole school of thought that believes that Paul didn't write the misogynistic parts of the Bible credited to him at all – that they were added later, years after his death, by men with a patriarchal and distinctly non-spiritual agenda. So I mentally dumped the misogyny from the Bible, along with all mentions of stoning people to death, homophobia, the Devil and sin. I focused on Jesus instead – after all, didn't he put the Christ into Christian?

My baptism went perfectly. My family came. The church was packed. A butterfly fluttered in the beams of autumn sunlight streaming through the windows. We sang my favourite hymn of all, 'Amazing Grace'. Then it was time for the baptism itself.

Props to the minister, after the whole women-should-submit-to-their-wives hoo-ha, he'd asked a woman to help baptise me. I appreciated the gesture but nothing could remove the terror of being dunked under water. A childhood swimming pool mishap had left me with a morbid fear of drowning and to this day I'm still not able to swim. I emerged from my dunking coughing and spluttering but mercifully still alive. It was when I was back at my pew and we all starting singing 'How Great Thou Art' that the highlight of the day happened. The butterfly that had been flying high above the stage at the front of the church suddenly made a beeline for me, landing on my arm, where it stayed for the duration of the song. That's at least *three whole minutes*. I don't know about you, but I've never been so close to a butterfly for so long before. I've never had one land on me for even a second. As I looked at the butterfly and the intricate red and black markings on its wings, I felt connected to everyone and everything. It was beautiful. Sadly, my niece, who was standing next to me, didn't share my joy. It turns out she's as petrified of butterflies as I am of water, so she spent the entire song in a state of terror.

Unfortunately, my baptism would be the last time I would feel truly happy and at peace in church. Over the next couple of months the cracks in my Christian faith began to widen. I continued to struggle with a lot of the fear-based rhetoric and felt increasingly alone. Then a friend took me to a Buddhist monastery in the heart of the countryside near the village. I'd gone with the mindset of a spectator, a spiritual tourist if you like, but as soon as I sat down on the floor of the temple and closed my eyes to meditate, something really strange happened. I felt exactly the same powerful connection to a place of peace and Love that I did in the Christian church. But how could this be? At the Christian church we often sang a song with the lyric 'Our God is greater than any other' and were frequently told that ours was the one true way. So why was I feeling exactly the same sense of peace and connection in a Buddhist temple? Of course, through my pub-lunch discussions with my dad, I had a strong hunch that I already knew the answer: that there was just one source of spiritual Love and many different routes to the same destination. Realising that I could access this Love anywhere was liberating to me. The truth was, I was embarrassed to call myself a Christian. I'd seen at close hand how hurt my gay friends had been by the Christian faith, and as a woman I felt that my integrity was constantly being compromised by the misogynistic teachings in the Bible. A couple of weeks later I left the Christian church for good.

Something More

Walking away from judgement

Judgement in any form is corrosive to our inner peace – and this applies whether we're the ones being judged or those doing the judging. If you've been affected by judgement try this simple exercise in letting go and healing the pain.

Set out on a walk to a specific destination at least twenty minutes away, preferably more. Set out with the intention that on the way to your destination you're going to shed your feelings of judgement, or the pain of being judged, like a snake sheds old skin. As you walk, picture the judgements you've been making or that have been made about you being cast off in your wake. When you arrive at the destination take a moment to revel in the feeling of lightness letting go brings. If you want to really process the experience, write down how you are feeling in your journal. When you're ready, set off back home, this time with the intention that you're walking to a brighter, more loving future. As you walk think about how you can fill the space left by the absence of judgement or the pain it causes with happier, more loving things. Mentally compile a list of things you're grateful for. Ask yourself how you can add to the love in the world. Take a moment to observe your surroundings and any joy they might bring.

Journal on judgement

Judgement, whether it comes from an establishment like the Church or an individual, always tends to be rooted in fear.

If you're being judged or judging someone else, try writing about the fear that might be causing it in your journal. Then write about how this insight can help you move away from judging others, or the pain of being judged.

6

SACRED FEMININE

*I am changed into that which I love more than myself,
that is, into Love, for I love nothing but Love.*

MARGUERITE PORETE

I don't want to be a bit-player when it comes to spirituality. I don't want to be made to feel ashamed, sidelined or silenced simply because I was born with a vagina. I don't want to be patronised or made to play small just because my body isn't in possession of a Y chromosome. I don't want to be consigned to making the tea, working in the Sunday school or clapping the men on from the wings. I want to be out there, preaching, teaching and blazing a trail for Love. I don't want to choose between being a virgin or a whore – because that's a choice born out of fear, created by the patriarchy. I want to celebrate my passion, my fire and my sensuality – just as I celebrate my humility. I don't want to be meek and mild – I want to be meek and *wild*. And I want to reclaim the sacred in the feminine. Shortly after leaving the Christian Church I wrote this poem:

Barefoot, Burning Love . . .
a poem of reclamation

When the Church photo-shopped women
Into virgins, sinners or whores
And told them they must be led
And must not speak,
Love kicked off Her shoes and
Danced out of the dogma,
Calling over Her shoulder,
'If you want me you can find me
Running barefoot in the forest,
Swimming naked in the stream.
Burning between a woman's legs,
Living wild among her dreams.'

This, to me, is the nub of it. There's nothing loving about oppressing or sidelining an entire gender. As far as I'm concerned, when you tell an entire section of society they're not as worthy as the rest, Love has left the building. Like someone emerging from a psychologically abusive relationship, I left the Church overwhelmed by the need to reclaim my sense of self, in this case as a female spiritual being. As luck would have it, I didn't have long to wait.

A friend invited me to a women's business conference she was speaking at in London. I turned up expecting talk of 'ball-breaking in the boardroom', 'idea showers' and 'blue-sky thinking'. I certainly wasn't expecting talk of the sacred feminine, but what unfurled was beyond my wildest dreams. In the introductory talk the conference organiser said that she believed women were wrong to try and copy men when it came to succeeding in business, because women are different from men and we should be proud of this. Instantly my hackles rose as I had visions of us being told that we ought to bring cupcakes to business meetings and should always wear pink, in some kind of nightmarish Tony Robbins/Stepford Wives mash-up. But she went on to explain that patriarchal societies and religions had conditioned us to view traditionally feminine qualities, such as empathy, emotions and intuition, as bad or weak, but that actually the reverse was true. It was time to reclaim what it meant to be a woman and play to our own unique strengths.

It can be easy to assume that the current way of the world is the way it's always been; that male gods and patriarchal societies and religions are just the way of things. However, nothing could be further from the truth. In fact, this way of doing things only accounts for a small portion of history. There was a time when women were respected and treated as equal within cultures and this was reflected in their divinity, with both gods and goddesses being worshipped.

The next speaker at the conference talked about how attitudes to women spiritually have changed over the centuries, using the menstrual cycle to highlight this. I jotted down copious notes as she gave a fascinating talk about how indigenous cultures, such as that of the Native Americans, viewed menstruation as a sacred thing, linked to the power of the moon. When Native American women were having their periods they were seen to be at the peak of their goddess energy and were sent to stay in 'Moon Lodges'. The purpose of these lodges was to give women time to go inwards, reconnect with themselves and release any pain they might be in. While in Moon Lodges women were believed to be at the height of their intuitive powers and often spoke great prophecies. Indigenous people also revered the menstrual blood itself, offering it to the gods as a gift and using it as a magical form of protection.

I think my mouth might have literally been hanging open in shock at this point. Like most women today, I'd been raised to see my periods as a complete pain and something to be hidden away like a dirty secret. At those awkward moments when we do have to mention the fact that we've got our period, it's always in some kind of weird code and hushed tones, such as: 'It's my time of the month' or 'I'm on at the moment'. Many women even refer to their periods as 'the curse'.

'Imagine if periods were treated in this way today,' the conference speaker continued. 'Imagine if menstruating women were shown the same kind of reverence.'

I pictured turning up at the publishing company I was freelancing for at the time, demanding that my male bosses build me a Moon Lodge to retreat to once a month; or even just a chill-out room with a bit of Marvin Gaye and some scented candles – I'm not fussy. It felt laughable, but why? A switch in my brain had been flicked. I loved the notion of seeing my monthly cycle as a spiritual thing, something magical and mystical, influenced by the moon. In ancient mythology, the female and moon cycles were completely intertwined, with each of the four phases of the moon seen as representing one of four female archetypes.

1. The *Maiden* archetype and a woman's pre-ovulation phase is represented by the growing energies of a waxing moon.

2. The *Mother* archetype and a woman's ovulation is represented by the abundant energy of a full moon.

3. The *Enchantress* archetype and the decreasing energies of the pre-menstrual phase is represented by a waning moon.

4. The *Crone* archetype and the menstrual phase is represented by the dark moon, the one to three days in every cycle when the moon isn't visible.

It's believed that the first calendars ever invented were based on women's charts of their menstrual cycles and moon cycles, with each year having thirteen months of twenty-eight days. It wasn't until the advent of Christianity that the calendar became solar based (the sun traditionally being linked to a masculine deity). In the second part of her talk, the conference speaker shared ways in which we could honour our own cycles, applying this specifically to our careers, charting the best times of the month to launch new projects, and capitalising on our peak energy and the times we needed to rest and replenish. Of course, in a world that deems female cycles a dirty secret, this is a luxury very few of us are afforded.

The next speaker at the conference talked about tapping into our wisdom as women, or as she put it, 'our crone energy'. At the mention of the word crone, I instinctively winced, picturing a shrivelled-up witch cackling over her cauldron – and yet this archetype is meant to embody an older woman's wisdom. The fact that we've been conditioned to see the archetype of female wisdom as something evil and to be feared is yet another example of how society and more specifically, religion, has systematically demeaned and disenfranchised women. It was wonderful to hear talk of reclaiming this wisdom at the conference. The speaker explained that crone energy represents the need to withdraw from the world and go inwards, so that we can tap into the wisdom and intuition found in stillness. The optimum time for this during the moon cycle is the dark of the moon, and the optimum time for tapping into this wisdom in a woman's cycle is during her period. It felt so empowering to think of the waning energy women experience at this time as a good thing; as a call to ramp up our meditation practice and reconnect to our soul.

I came home from the conference on a mission. I was determined to find out more about the sacred feminine and how she'd been airbrushed from history. The first step on my mission was to find out why attitudes to women's periods had changed so drastically, from something sacred and revered to something shameful and unclean. What I found made for some pretty disturbing reading, with all of the current major world religions guilty to some degree.

In Judaism, a woman is considered *niddah* or impure for up to two weeks of the month. This phase begins with her period and ends a full week after her period has ended, when she must undergo an elaborate bath ritual known as *mikveh*. This tradition is rooted in Leviticus 15, from the Old Testament:

When a woman has her regular flow of blood, the impurity of her monthly period will last seven days, and anyone who touches her will be unclean till evening. Anything she lies on during her period will be unclean, and anything she sits on will be unclean. Anyone who touches her bed will be unclean; they must wash their clothes and bathe with water, and they will be unclean till evening. Anyone who touches anything she sits on will be unclean; they must wash their clothes and bathe with water, and they will be unclean till evening. Whether it is the bed or anything she was sitting on, when anyone touches it, they will be unclean till evening. If a man has sexual relations with her and her monthly flow touches him, he will be unclean for seven days; any bed he lies on will be unclean.

In the Eastern Orthodox Christian Church, women are banned from receiving communion during their periods. In Islam a menstruating woman mustn't have sex, touch the Quran or go to a mosque. In Hinduism, menstruation is seen as a spiritual as well as physical impurity and women were – and still are in some parts of the world – banned from touching other people or speaking loudly, and banished to a hut until their period was over, and not in a positive 'Moon Lodge' way. Thankfully, I hadn't been brought up with any of these traditions, but I'd still absorbed the lesson from society that periods are unclean, with tampons and towels labelled 'women's sanitary protection' in stores. I wondered how different my life and every other woman's might have been if we'd been taught to see our monthly cycles as a sacred thing and actively encouraged to take regular time to honour our body's needs and go within. How amazing it would be if tampons and towels were placed in a 'women's *sacred* protection' section in stores, along with candles, journals and incense, and anything else that might help us tap into our inner wisdom. If only there were other women out there who wanted to reclaim this sacred aspect of the feminine.

It turns out that there are, in the small but growing Red Tent movement, inspired by the bestselling novel *The Red Tent* by Anita Diamant. *The Red Tent* is a fictional account of the story of Dinah from the Old Testament. Like all women in the Bible,

Dinah's story is of the 'blink and you'll miss it' variety. In a nutshell, Dinah, the daughter of Leah and Jacob, is raped by a man called Shechem, who then decides that she's so attractive he'd actually like to marry her. Lucky Dinah. Diamant reimagines this story from Dinah's perspective, with the red tent of the title referring to the tents women in those times (around 1500 BC) would be sent to during menstruation and childbirth. Diamant imagines the support, advice and life wisdom that would have been shared among the tribe's women in the red tent, from one generation to the next. The modern day Red Tent movement tries to replicate this experience, with monthly meetings for women at the time of a new, full or dark moon. A common feature of these groups is a 'sharing circle' where the women take it in turns to talk about whatever is on their mind. One thing that comes up time and again when you read interviews or quotes from participants is the luxury of women being fully witnessed and listened to in these circles, and what a novel experience this can be for most of them.

I was so inspired by this that I decided to try a get-together of my own with a group of female friends. Rather than investing in a tent, I invited them to my flat one Friday evening – it was the middle of winter, after all, peak crone season but bitterly cold. Not wanting to scare away my guests with talk of sacred menstrual blood, I called the gathering a 'Women's Night of Wit, Wine and Wisdom', and made a very general reference to a tradition I'd read about where women came together to share stories from their lives. I prepared a hearty buffet-style feast and baked a 'wisdom cake' – chocolate and raspberry in case you're interested, my definition of a wise flavour combination. We sat in a circle, picnic style, on my living room floor, with the food laid out in the middle on a blanket, and we each took turns to speak. There were no guidelines about what we should speak about. The only rule was that anything goes. I kicked things off as I was still mildly traumatised by a discovery I'd made on the internet earlier about something called the perimenopause. Obviously, I'd heard of the menopause before – although not a lot because that seems to be deemed even more shameful than periods – but I had no idea that most women also experience a kind of menopause warm-up act, which in some cases can last for ten years, and include such delights as insomnia, mood swings, vaginal dryness and urine leakage when coughing or sneezing.

'Why had I never heard of this before?' I asked the group. 'Why does nobody talk about it?'

'I only just found out about it too,' one of my friends said.

'I think I'm having mine,' said another, 'I've been having some crazy mood swings.'

This then triggered a general bitch about how rubbish it was to be a woman.

'As if it's not bad enough having periods for years – we can't even end them without going through hell,' one of my friends moaned.

I thought back to our ancient ancestors and how they honoured every cycle in a woman's life. If we'd been born back then we wouldn't have been having this conversation. Tribal cultures don't even have a word for the menopause because it's seen as such a natural thing; a graceful transition into becoming one of the tribe's wise elders, an essential part of the rhythm of all things. Back in the day an older woman's wisdom was revered in spiritual circles. In ancient Greece the older aspect of the woman was seen as the goddess Sophia, representing wisdom. In the Celtic tradition the goddess Cerridwen was seen as a sage old woman, past child-bearing age, linked to the dark moon and known for her cauldron of wisdom. Cerridwen's message was that something must die in order for rebirth and this is how the menopause was once seen; the end of a long cycle of menstruating, giving birth to a profound spiritual change, as a woman's wisdom and affinity with the moon's cycles deepens. When seen in a spiritual light, any tiredness and physical discomfort a woman might feel during this time is something to be celebrated and embraced as an essential part of the process. The menopause was seen as a time of retreat, contemplation and healing – a spiritual opportunity to let go of the old to make way for the new, and step into a deeper wisdom.

As my friends and I ate cake, drank wine and shared the intimate, vulnerable and funny stories from our lives, we also shared our support, advice and love. By the end of the night there was a palpable sense that we were all a lot happier, and our friendships had deepened. The benefits of having a gathering like this on a monthly basis honouring our sacred femininity seemed immeasurable.

SACRED MISSING PERSON'S GALLERY

In the years I've been researching the sacred feminine, I've discovered a missing person's gallery of goddesses, saints, mystics and poets who have been all but airbrushed from history. Here are a just a few of my favourites.

Thecla

The chances are that you've never heard of Thecla. I hadn't until very recently. But in the first few centuries after Jesus's death she was a household name, in Christian households at least, with pilgrims flocking to her shrines and revering her as one of the most important people outside the Holy Trinity. Thecla's story is told in *The Acts of Paul and Thecla* (a text dating back to the second century, although some scholars have dated it as early as AD 70). The text is one of many gospels and scriptures that early Christians saw as sacred, but they didn't make the grade when a council (all-male) in Rome decided what should go into the New Testament, some three hundred years after Jesus's death. Thecla's story begins when the apostle Paul arrives in her home city of Iconium, in Asia Minor, and begins preaching his message from her next-door neighbour's house.

Seventeen-year-old Thecla sat spellbound in her window for three days and nights listening to Paul's message, which focused heavily on sexual renunciation: 'Blessed are those who have kept the flesh chaste, for they will become a temple of God' (Acts of Thecla 5). Thecla's mother was not very impressed by this as she'd just arranged for her daughter to be married to a man named Thamyris. Back then arranged marriages were the norm, with women having no say in things and very few rights at all. But Thecla would not be moved. Paul's words had convinced her to renounce sex and devote herself to God. Thamyris was outraged at this turn of events and dragged Paul off to the governor of the city to stand trial. That night, Thecla managed to bribe her way into Paul's cell, where she spent the night listening to his eloquent words and 'kissing his bonds' – not a euphemism. Paul and Thecla were both sent to trial. As an outsider, Paul was flogged and banished from the city. As a local, Thecla was condemned to be burnt at the stake. But, just as the flames were taking hold, a divine intervention in the form of a freak thunderstorm extinguished them, and Thecla escaped. She tracked down Paul and begged him to allow her to join him on his mission, offering to cut off her hair so she would pass as a male. Paul, rather mean-spiritedly, some might say, refused to baptise Thecla, fearing that she might change her mind. But he allowed her to join him and they travelled to Antioch. When they arrived a prominent citizen named Alexander noticed Thecla and tried to force himself upon her. Rather than submitting to his will, Thecla tore off his cloak and crown, publicly humiliating him.

Although the gathered crowd found this highly amusing, Alexander had a serious sense of humour failure and took Thecla to the local magistrate, who condemned her to be thrown to her death in an arena of wild animals. Many local women protested the great injustice of this sentence, but to no avail. There then followed a series of scenes straight from an epic action film. First, a wild lioness was unleashed on Thecla but instead of killing her, she licked her feet and killed the bear that was subsequently sent to kill her. But as more and more wild animals were released into the arena, Thecla began to despair. Spotting a vat filled with human-eating seals (yes, really), Thecla threw herself into the water and baptised herself. At this point, God once again intervened, this time with a lightning bolt, which killed the seals and allowed Thecla to escape. Realising he was fighting a losing battle, the governor then gave up and released her. Thecla dressed as a man and set off to find Paul. When she found him, he told her to go and teach the word of God. She spent the rest of her life preaching the Christian gospel.

Now, I can guess what you're thinking – human-eating seals, convenient thunder and lightning storms, feet-licking lionesses – it's all a tad far-fetched, but taken in the context of the miracle stories the Bible is crammed full of, the story of Thecla is no more or less believable. What it does do is give women and girls a strong spiritual heroine they can look up to – a woman who, thousands of years before the #MeToo movement, wouldn't be sold off to a man, or humiliated or raped by one; a woman who wanted to devote her life to her spiritual faith and when a man wouldn't baptise her, she baptised herself – in a vat full of murderous sea-life creatures, no less. No wonder she was a household name in the first few centuries of Christianity. Imagine being taught that story in Sunday school. Imagine a Thecla-inspired sermon about the importance of owning your own power. Imagine Christian boys, girls, women and men growing up to believe that *none* of us needs permission when it comes to fiercely devoting ourselves to Love, and that both men *and* women can be spiritual leaders.

Brigid

Brigid was a goddess in pre-Christian Ireland, known as the patron of poetry, medicine, arts and crafts – most specifically blacksmithing – livestock, sacred wells, the eternal flame and the arrival of spring. She is the goddess of the elevated state and wisdom. All in all, it's a pretty impressive job description. Her feast day is known as Imbolc, and is on 1 February, the very first day of spring, so Brigid represents the first ray of light after a long period of darkness. My favourite story about Brigid is that she made the first-ever whistle, to be used by people as a way of calling out to each other as they walked through the night, a much-needed reminder that they weren't alone.

Kali

Kali is a Hindu goddess depicted with four arms. In one hand she brandishes a sword, in another a severed head. Kali represents the destruction that is essential for growth. Although she looks pretty menacing, she's not meant to be feared. Her other two hands are depicted in the *mudras* (spiritual gestures) representing fearlessness and blessings. The severed head she holds is meant to represent the death of the ego. Kali is a great goddess to call upon if you need help clearing out the dead wood in your life, whether that be an unfulfilling job, an abusive relationship, or negative thoughts or behaviours, and is another powerful representation of the sacred feminine.

Marguerite Porete

Marguerite Porete was a French mystic born in the thirteenth century. She was a member of the Beguine Order, a semi-monastic Christian community, members of which didn't take vows and were free to leave at any time. The Beguines modelled themselves on Christ's life, taking care of the poor and the sick, and devoting themselves to God. In the 1290s Marguerite Porete wrote a book called *The Mirror of Simple Souls*, in which she talked about how she believed that it was possible to unite with divine Love and become that Love itself. This did not go down well with the Christian institution as the implication was that it was surplus to requirement. So, after a lengthy trial, Marguerite was burnt at the stake in Paris in 1310 for refusing to deny her views or remove her book from circulation. It's easy to skim over stories like these, dismissing them as dusty relics from history, but think of the huge amounts of courage this required. Here was a woman who believed so passionately in spiritual Love as a universal thing – something we all are capable of experiencing without the authority of the Church – that she was willing to die an unimaginably horrible death for it. Hundreds of years later, her book is still in print and is regarded as a spiritual classic.

Something More

Moon circle

If you'd like to reclaim the sacred feminine, why not host your own moon gathering? Serve food – I highly recommend some kind of wisdom cake (see page 74) – and invite a group of your friends who will be open to this kind of thing. Invite your guests to take it in turns to share anything that might be on their minds, and instruct the others to witness and listen. If it goes well, why not open up your event to the public? You could, for instance, create a private Facebook group so members of your circle can share and support each other online too.

Brigid meditation

If you've recently been through a difficult or dark time, try meditating to Brigid. Light a candle to symbolise Brigid's eternal flame. Slow your breathing and focus your gaze on the flame. Realise that no matter how dark things have been, the light, like the sun, is always there – it's just that sometimes it gets obscured by the clouds of our depression, anxiety or fear. If it helps, repeat the following mantra out loud or in your head: 'I welcome the light into my life.' Afterwards, note down in your journal how your life could be lighter, and any evidence of the first buds of spring.

The dance of Kali

Put on some music that you find empowering and inspiring, something with a good, strong beat, and dance, pretending your arm is a scythe. Visualise yourself hacking away at anything that's currently holding you back. Tap into the divine feminine within you. Feel her formidable strength. Feel your formidable strength. Hack away with your arms until you feel free from burden. Then dance into the resulting space. Feel your body become as light as air. Float on the rhythm. Enjoy the freedom and space that comes with the destruction of things that no longer serve you. Revel in the feeling that spiritual Love is just as much feminine as it is masculine. Really feel this in the core of your body.

7

DIVINE DANCE CLASS

Dancing is when you rise above both worlds, tearing your heart into pieces and giving up your soul.

RUMI

Like so many of the gifts I received on my quest for Something More, my discovery that dance could be a spiritual practice happened entirely by accident. When I first moved to the village I made a list of possible ways in which I could make new, local friends. 'Join a dance class' was at the top. I'd always harboured a secret passion for dance. As a child I devoured the TV series *Fame* and wished more than anything that I too could go to dance school and live in a legwarmer-clad world where spontaneously breaking into choreographed routines was de rigueur. I'd seen a sign advertising a dance class at my local town hall for weeks before I actually plucked up the courage to go. 'Biodanza. Come and join the dance of life', the sign said. As the class took place every Wednesday morning I was expecting it to be full of the wealthy mums who lived in the town and seemed to spend their lives shuttling between beauty salons, coffee shops and yoga. But when I arrived at the ornate town hall I was surprised to see a real cross section of people. For a start there were a fair few men, and the ages ranged from thirty to sixty-something. The teacher, a lovely welcoming woman named Pip, came over to greet me.

'Have you done Biodanza before?' she asked.

I shook my head.

'It's quite different to any other kind of dance class,' she said. 'But don't worry, there are no steps to learn.'

As far as I was concerned this was very good indeed. I might have harboured Kids from *Fame* fantasies but when it came to choreography, I had two left feet.

The class began with us all holding hands in a circle and slowly stepping round to the right. At first I felt extremely self-conscious – I hadn't had to hold hands in a circle since I was a child. But everyone seemed super-friendly and as the track went on I relaxed into it. Next, a more upbeat song came on and we were told to 'walk free'. This basically involved walking around the large room in as carefree a way as possible. Midway through the track I saw Pip begin to skip and I couldn't help following suit. I hadn't skipped since I was a child either and it was exhilarating. By the end of the track I was skipping around the room with my arms spread wide, the way my friends and I used to do when we were pretending to be aeroplanes. Then the dancing began. For some tracks we were instructed to dance in pairs, for others we could dance alone. At the beginning of each dance, Pip would do a short demonstration and there would usually be some kind of direction, like 'Tune in to your partner's rhythm, be really present for them,' or 'Dance yourself free from stress.' My favourite was a tribal dance we did to a piece of African music. The rhythm of the drums was hypnotic and I felt myself sinking into my feet, with all of my worries being pounded into the ground. By this point my initial feelings of awkwardness had totally disappeared. Biodanza was nothing like I had expected, but it was definitely a pleasant and interesting surprise.

In the final section of the class the tempo of the music slowed and things became much more contemplative. We had to do a 'breathing dance' to a haunting track by Enya. This involved standing rooted to the spot with our eyes closed, moving our arms very slowly in and out, in time with our breath. It was a powerful experience, like a deep meditation, and it was the first time I realised that you didn't have to be sitting in stillness to feel connected to Something More. Halfway through the dance my eyes filled with tears. I didn't have a clue why this happened, I just felt deeply moved. We finished the class with a final circle. This time when we held hands I didn't feel any awkwardness. Dancing had dissolved away our barriers and I felt completely connected to all the other members of the group.

I started going dancing every week, and every week the same thing would happen. We'd all trudge into the room carrying the weight of the week's worries on our shoulders, but then we'd start dancing and within minutes we'd be like joyful children, skipping, laughing and fooling around. It turned out that there was a science behind this. Biodanza, which translated means 'the dance of life', was created in the 1960s by a Chilean psychologist named Rolando Toro. He had been fascinated by the impact of music and movement on a person's emotional as well as physical well-being. Every class and the music featured is carefully planned with the intention of building self-esteem, encouraging the expression of emotions and improving people's connection with others.

I was discovering another, unexpected bonus; when I lost myself in the dance I found a deeper connection to Something More. Able to quieten my mind to the music, I could tap into the same source of inner peace and wisdom I'd found in meditation and in church. Dance to me had become a form of prayer. What I didn't realise then was that historically, many cultures and spiritual faiths have used dance as a way of connecting to the divine. Perhaps the best known of these are the whirling dervishes of Sufism.

My dad had recently introduced me to Sufism at our 'Church of Pub Lunches'. Sufism is a mystical branch of Islam. Possibly the best-known Sufi, in the West at least, is Jalal ad-Din Rumi. He was born in what is now Afghanistan in 1207. When the Mongols invaded Rumi's family fled, finally settling in Konya, Turkey. As an adult Rumi was an orthodox religious scholar until, at the age of thirty-seven, he met a wandering dervish called Shams of Tabriz, who introduced Rumi to the concept of music, poetry and dance being used as a way of connecting to the divine. The two men became inseparable friends and spiritual confidantes. They were so close that when Shams died, Rumi believed he was channelling his spirit in his poetry.

The more I read about Rumi, the more I became intrigued by the way he and his followers – the Melevi Order – had used a whirling form of dance as a way of connecting to God. I'd heard of whirling dervishes before but my knowledge of them was seriously limited. I'd assumed they liked dancing round and round in circles purely for the fun of it. I had no idea that their dance was so loaded with spiritual symbolism.

The Melevi's Sema ceremony, for which they are probably best known and which was said to have been created by Rumi himself, is carefully choreographed to be a spiritual practice. Even the clothes they wear have spiritual meaning. The camel-hair hats worn by the dancers represent the tombstone of the ego, and their billowing white skirts the ego's shroud. When the dancers take off their black cloaks it symbolises their spiritual rebirth into the truth. When they cross their arms over their chests, denoting the number one, this symbolises God's unity. The drumbeat at the beginning of the ceremony represents God's command 'Be' for the creation of the universe. The subsequent improvisation on the reed flute represents life-giving breath.

The dancers then make a circular procession three times, anti-clockwise, to symbolise the three stages of knowledge: the things we learn through study, those we learn through observation and those we learn through experience. Then the dancing begins, with separate movements exploring different religious themes. As the dancers spin they are embracing the entire universe. When they raise their right hands they are receiving gifts from God. When they extend their left hands downwards they are distributing these divine gifts to the rest of humanity. Reading about the whirling dervishes gave credence to my own, home-made spiritual practice through dance and I embraced this new, physical way of connecting to Something More.

At around the time I left the Christian Church, Pip and a couple of her colleagues set up a teacher-training school in London. She urged me to enrol on the three-year course.

'Even if you never end up teaching Biodanza you'll get so much from it on a personal level,' she told me. 'I can guarantee you'll be so much happier.'

I was already getting so much from my dance practice that it didn't take much to convince me. The teacher training involved going to Richmond for one weekend every month. Each day of the weekend would begin with a theory session, where we learnt the science behind the different dances and the carefully chosen music. Then we would have two dance sessions, broken up by a group meal, where we'd all bring food to share.

The first day of the school was an incredible experience that I'll never forget. There were students there from all over the world – Brazil, Venezuela, Germany, France, Holland – as well as the four corners of the UK. When we danced together for the first time it was like being at a rave – but without the addition of artificial stimulants. There was so much joy in the room, and doing two dance sessions back to back deepened my feeling of spiritual connection. Expressing Love and gratitude through my dance made it all the more powerful.

When I finally got home that night I was still on a high, despite the three-hour train journey. As I took Max out for a midnight stroll around the village, I cranked up the volume on my iPod. I didn't want the music to end. We reached Max's favourite clearing and he went for a sniff of the towering pine trees, and I gazed up into the night sky. It was ablaze with stars and a huge full moon shimmered silver. I thought of ancient cultures and how they'd seen the divine in everything – the moon, the trees, the earth, the sky, themselves. This was exactly how I felt in that moment, part of an exquisite divine tapestry. And I *still* wanted to dance. At exactly that moment George Michael's 'Fast Love' came on my iPod shuffle, and before I knew it I was dancing around the clearing. I'd like to point out again here that no alcohol or other substances had been consumed. I felt full of unadulterated joy – and more certain than ever of the existence of Something More, permeating everything. And then . . .

'Bloody hell, it's like being back in Thailand!'

I spun around to see a guy on the footpath behind me.

Previously, I would have been mortified at being caught dancing on my own in the middle of the village in the middle of the night like this. No, scrap that. Previously, I would *never* have been dancing on my own in the middle of the night in the middle of the village like this. But dancing as some kind of spiritual practice was melting away my inhibitions as well as my worries and fears. I took out my earbuds and started to laugh.

'Sorry, I was just – er – dancing to George Michael.' Sadly, dancing as a spiritual practice had done nothing for my conversational skills.

The guy chuckled. 'For a moment there I thought I was back at a full moon party.'

At this point my furry guardian angel Max came running over and gave the guy a cautionary growl.

'Night then,' he said. 'Have fun!'

'I will.'

When I got into bed that night it felt as if every fibre in my body was still dancing. I'd been told that the teacher training would take us deep, and several people had mentioned that due to the therapeutic nature of the classes, issues were likely to come up. The philosophy behind Biodanza is that you don't need to talk about these issues, you just dance them out. Talking during class – unless absolutely necessary – is actually banned. So sometimes you would hear sniffing, sometimes full-on sobs. But we all kept dancing, allowing the person the space to work through whatever was coming up for them on their own.

I know it's probably hard to grasp how a dance class could

trigger emotional issues, so let me give you a couple of examples of how this might happen. Sometimes we'd be told to dance in threes. Now, I don't care what De la Soul said, three is not always a magic number. To anyone who has abandonment or jealousy issues, the number three can trigger deep-rooted inse-curities. In the dance sessions this could occur if you felt that the other two people were paying more attention to each other than to you. Sometimes we'd be asked to choose a partner to dance with and if there was an odd number of people in the class, you could be left dancing on your own. To anyone who was always the last to be picked for teams in PE or had any kind of rejec-tion issues, this scenario could also be extremely painful. Time and again during the teacher-training weekends people would encounter issues on the dance floor. But the great thing was that this gave you the opportunity to work through these issues in a safe space and express your feelings through the dance.

The thing that came up for me was self-love, or rather lack of it. Ever since encountering the Jesus quote about loving your neighbour *as yourself* I'd been aware that self-love was key to spiritual growth, but it was something I still hadn't quite cracked. Of course, it didn't help that loving oneself is so often seen as being an arrogant thing to do. But I think that Jesus stressed the importance of loving ourselves because he saw that it was an essential prerequisite of being able to love others. Think about it for a moment. If you harbour feelings of self-loathing or inadequacy there's no well of Love inside you to draw upon. Sure, you can go through the motions, telling people you love them and acting as if you do, but ultimately the feelings of self-hatred you've been harbouring will spill over into anger, resentment and a need to withdraw, or even worse, lash out. My issues dated back to events in my childhood that had left me convinced I wasn't lovable. The problem with childhood trauma is that children just don't have the wisdom and experience to be able to see things for what they truly are. If someone hurts us when we're a child, we internalise the pain and all too often absorb the false message that we are to blame. And when I'd begun my quest for Something More, the instinct to seek external validation, either through my relationship status or career achievements, was still there. I was still searching for healing outside myself.

So I developed a bit of a crush on one of the guys at the school. On the face of it he was the very worst person to have a crush on. He was charming, funny, great company – and totally unavailable. I don't mean that he was with someone else, it was more that he was an incorrigible flirt who liked to share his charms with all and sundry. The emotionally unavailable can be irresistible for someone needing to prove their lovability. *If I can get a guy who plays the field to like me, then I'll really prove I'm lovable,* so the effed-up logic goes, as if they're some perverse version of a Scrabble triple letter score. Sadly, despite my growing spiritual practice, I still had work to do – but luckily it turned out that I'd discovered the best place in the world to do it in.

Here's what would happen: some weekends I'd rock up at the school and the guy would be all over me. We'd dance together and the attraction between us would feel intense. Then the very next day, he'd turned from hot to cold and would be pouring his attentions all over another woman. I felt disproportionately affected by this – caught up in a roller coaster of highs and lows. Looking back now I can see that it was nothing to do with him personally. It was more that he'd come to symbolise a lifelong fear and I was stuck in some nightmare musical version of *Groundhog Day*, forced to repeat the painful experience over and over again.

Then one sweet day I had a breakthrough. I'd been feeling really low about things, annoyed that having come so far and been feeling so happy in my spiritual practice, I'd got myself in a situation that was making me feel rubbish again. As we did a dance designed to tap into the energy of fire I lost myself in the pounding rhythm and began to pray – *really* pray, with my whole being. I thought of the women who'd gone before me – the poets and mystics and free spirits, who'd been burnt at the stake for their spiritual beliefs. I prayed that I too might tap into this strength and this unshakeable faith; that I could finally be free from the spectre of fear that haunted me. As my prayer and body and the music became one, I felt primal and powerful and raw. I felt a love like fire burning all the fear away. Suddenly, my dance-floor crush and the need to prove my lovability seemed so silly. I'd prayed and danced myself to a place where ego fears simply didn't exist; a place that no amount of life coaching, counselling or self-help books with naff titles had been able to help me reach. As sweat poured down my face I felt connected to women from centuries before me, dancing around fires, beneath the moon, their souls aflame. I felt wild and feminine, fierce and divine. I felt Love in its purest form and best of all, it was coming from inside me. Dancing my prayer had set me free.

Something More

Breathing dance

Choose a very slow and gentle piece of music – 'Watermark' by Enya is perfect for this. Standing in bare feet, with your eyes closed, take a moment to get grounded in your body, placing one hand on your belly and the other on your chest. Take a couple of slow, deep breaths. Then on your next in-breath, slowly extend your arms up and out until your heart is wide open. As you slowly exhale, bring your hands back in to your chest. Repeat this movement for the rest of the track, keeping your eyes closed throughout, only moving your arms, as you slowly dance to your breath. Repeat the track if necessary until you feel your mind quieten and your body completely relax. Once you've completed the breathing dance write down any observations you might have had in your journal.

Shake out your fears

If you feel you have a residue of fear, anger, regret or any other negative emotion trapped inside you, try shaking it free to a piece of up-tempo music ('Shake it Out' by Florence and the Machine and 'Shake it Off' by Taylor Swift are perfect tracks for this exercise). Start with your feet firmly planted on the floor and begin shaking your hands. Then extend the shaking to your arms and shoulders. Next stand on one leg and shake out the other, swapping legs after about thirty seconds. Then shake your belly and your hips. Finally, shake

all over, free-style to the music. As you shake your body picture yourself getting rid of your negative emotions into the
air and on to the floor. Keep doing the shaking dance until
your body and mind feel lighter. When animals experience
trauma they may shake violently for a few moments as a form
of release. Then they trot off and get on with the business
of being a deer, rabbit or whatever again, with no need for
a Ben & Jerry's fest or months in therapy. This exercise is a
great way of tapping into this animal wisdom, freeing us from
the stagnant feelings that block us from love.

8

FROM WONDER TO GRATITUDE

Never once in my life did I ask God for
success or wisdom or power or fame. I asked
for wonder and he gave it to me.

ABRAHAM JOSHUA HESCHEL

In his book *Who is Man?* Jewish theologian Abraham Joshua Heschel writes: 'Wonder, or radical amazement, is a way of going beyond what is given in thing and thought, refusing to take anything for granted, to regard anything as final. It is our honest response to the grandeur and mystery of reality, our confrontation with that which transcends the given.'

Firstly, don't you love the phrase 'radical amazement'? It makes me think of a group of people wandering through life, eyes saucer-wide, wearing T-shirts emblazoned with the words 'Radically Amazed!' and constantly *ooh*-ing and *aah*-ing in delighted surprise. It's definitely a club I'd join. There's so much in this life to get radically amazed about – so much grandeur and mystery. Just gaze up into a starry sky, study the intricate petals of a flower or listen to the sighs of the ocean. Or hold a baby, and touch their velvety new-born skin. Wonder at how this all came to be. Immerse yourself in a symphony by Mozart or drink in a Salvador Dali painting. Read the poems of Pablo Neruda or Insta-poet Atticus. Fall in love. Feel your soul crack open in the middle of your pain. There are reasons for wonder everywhere. And yet . . .

So many of us are so jaded and cynical. Instead of being radically amazed we're resolutely unfazed – and we wear our cynicism like a badge of honour. Just take a look on Twitter. Scroll through the sarcasm, bitterness and bile. See how quick people are to jump on a hashtag of hate. But don't stay there too long. Seriously. Don't. Hatred is toxic and it spreads fear. Instead of spending hours aimlessly scrolling through the negativity, take yourself offline and outside, and find a reason to be filled with wonder. Wonder is a gift that truly keeps on giving, but how is it a part of a spiritual practice?

While I was doing the Biodanza teacher training, I was invited to a dance workshop at a studio in the heart of London's Kings Cross. At the end of our lunch break one of the organisers told us that she was going to be holding a 'Mayaan cacao ceremony' before we began dancing again. She told us that it was what the ancient Mayaans did whenever they wanted to connect to the divine. As I watched her pour a thick, chocolatey drink into shot glasses my first response was one of my dad's favourite mantras – 'What a load of old bollocks.' I didn't say it out loud for the sake of politeness but it was certainly in the thought bubble over my head. Now, I love chocolate as much as the next person – probably even more – but how the hell could drinking some hot chocolate possibly connect you to God? The woman was wearing tie-dyed yoga pants too, and I've always had an irrational hatred of tie-dyed yoga pants. All of my bullshit alarms were ringing. But then my curiosity kicked in – it was the same curiosity that saw me smoking dope from a home-made bong at the age of fourteen. So I joined the circle and necked the drink. It was teeth-strippingly bitter and sludge thick. *Ha!* I thought to myself. *There's no way this is going to have any effect on me. It doesn't even taste nice!*

Fast-forward an hour into our dance class and I'd come to the mind-blowing realisation that the song 'Return to Innocence' by Enigma actually contained the secret to the meaning of life. Fast-forward another thirty minutes and I was head over heels in love with everyone in that room – including yoga-pants lady – because I'd realised that we're all one, man. Fast-forward another thirty minutes, to when the workshop was over, and I was sitting cross-legged on the pavement outside. I'd been overcome by the overwhelming urge to look at a tree. As the dance workshop was in a community centre on a council estate in London's Kings Cross, trees were in very short supply. But somehow I'd found one and I gazed up into it – suddenly acutely aware that the tree was me and I was the tree. This realisation made me extremely happy. Then I looked down at the pavement and spied a cigarette butt. I was overwhelmed with wonder at its beauty. For if God had created the tree and God had created me, then this cigarette butt was also part of the same divine tapestry.

Somehow, I made it on to the right train home. And somehow I managed to get off at the right station. Then I found myself walking along the canal back to the cottage. It was on the canal path that I had the dramatic realisation that trees were alive – *really alive*. And they could understand everything we said. So, I spent the next twenty minutes saying hello to every tree I walked past.

I finally got back to the cottage and felt the powerful urge to meditate. I sat down on the floor of the darkened living room and zoned out into a place of complete and utter peace. At some point my son, who hadn't heard me arrive home, came downstairs to get a drink. When he turned on the light and saw me sitting cross-legged in the dark he nearly passed out from shock.

'Mum! What are you doing?' he exclaimed.

'Thinking about talking to trees,' I replied.

'I thought you said taking drugs was wrong,' came his response.

'I haven't been taking drugs! I've just had some really strong hot chocolate.'

'Yeah, right.'

The next day I woke up with a case of the horrors as one by one, memories from the day before filled my mind. I quickly deleted a Facebook post I'd made at midnight, declaring 'Return to Innocence' to be the musical answer to the Question of Everything. I then deleted nine of the ten photographs of cigarette butts on my phone. I kept one to show my dad. I knew he'd appreciate the craic. He did more than that – he asked me if I could get hold of any of this cacao stuff and have it delivered to him in a brown paper bag. I think he was only half joking.

A Google search for Mayaan cacao ceremonies informed me that consuming ceremony-strength cacao 'takes you to the door of your awakening'. It also increases the blood flow to the brain by 30–40 per cent and the oxygen in your blood is increased by 20 per cent. Although I was clearly under the influence of a stimulant that day, the sense of wonder at the world it provoked in me lingered. Admittedly, I haven't felt any lasting love for cigarette butts, but my relationship with trees has definitely deepened.

Going back to the quote by Heschel at the beginning of this chapter, cultivating a sense of wonder at the world is a great way of recalibrating our mood and perspective on things. It's also a gateway to gratitude, a practice that is recommended time and again in different faith traditions. It's virtually impossible to be in awe of a stunning sunset, the majesty of the ocean or the beauty of a flower without instantly feeling thankful too. Like wonder, gratitude helps us to take a step back, to slip out from our ego's grasp and see our true place in things. Gratitude enables us to appreciate what a gift this life is and to see the gift in others too. It helps us to be more joyful. It can also help us overcome fear and return to a place of love. Let me give you an example from my own life – a cheery story I've called 'The Wailing Weekend'.

The Wailing Weekend took place shortly after my ex-husband and I broke up and he had moved in with another woman. My son was going to their house for the weekend, which meant that not only did I face the wrench of being apart from my child for two days, but I had a catalogue of images of them playing happy families to torture myself with. And torture myself I did. I pictured group hugs and bedtime stories and this new woman trying to take my place. She wasn't, of course, but when my imagination throws a pity party it really goes to town. So, it wasn't long before I was wailing on my tragic sofa *for one* and crying snotty tears into my tragic ready-meal *for one*. By day two of the weekend, I realised I needed an intervention and as

I was all alone – *oh, so alone* – I realised that it was down to me to do it. So I forced myself out of the house and up to London and into the biggest bookshop in town, where I figured they'd have the biggest self-help section in town, and if ever I needed to help myself it was now.

I desperately scanned the shelves for a book with a title like: *How to Survive the Heartbreak of Your Son Spending the Weekend with His Dad's New Family . . . and the Fear that He Might Never Want to Return*. Weirdly, I couldn't find one. But what I did find was a book I'd seen recommended on *Oprah* a few months before – *Simple Abundance: A Daybook of Comfort and Joy* by a writer called Sarah Ban Breathnach. It's a big book filled with warm-hearted wisdom, but it was one small exercise in it that ended up saving me from misery. And that small exercise was to write a daily gratitude list. Every night, before going to bed, Breathnach recommends writing a list of all the things that have happened that day that you're grateful for. At first, this was incredibly hard. How could I feel grateful for anything when I no longer got to spend every day with my young son, and when on the days he wasn't with me he was with *another woman*? But Breathnach urges that however hard you might find it, you need to list at least three things that you're grateful for, so that's what I did. I think my first gratitude list, written during that weekend, went something like this:

1. I'm grateful that at least I'm not dying from the bubonic plague.
2. I'm grateful that I don't have five children – then I'd be feeling five times as bad!
3. I'm grateful that . . .

I stuck with it, however, and after a while began to find genuine reasons to feel grateful. The lists usually involved food, or coffee, but at least it was a start. After a week or two something interesting happened – I started noticing things to feel grateful for *as they happened*, rather than when I was reflecting back on the events of the day. So, for example, if I had a really nice interaction with a person in a shop I'd make a mental note there and then to put it on my gratitude list that night. If I was eating a particularly delicious slice of cake I felt grateful for it as I was eating it, not just in retrospect. I started becoming attuned to gratitude and instead of looking for reasons to be sad, began seeking out reasons to be glad. This is the joy of a gratitude practice – it rewires your brain to seek out the good.

To make gratitude a truly spiritual practice you also need to regularly give thanks for the Something More that makes everything possible. Religious people give thanks to God. Personally, I give thanks to Love. In my mind Love and gratitude are inextricably linked. Gratitude is an acknowledgement of Love and an expression of it. It's a powerful antidote to toxins like fear and hate too – a spiritual antioxidant, if you like. And this is where we have to roll up our sleeves and get into the real heart of gratitude as a spiritual practice. It's easy to feel grateful for a cake, a rainbow, a sunset or a kiss, but how about feeling grateful for the difficult and painful things life throws at us? How about feeling grateful for the messy divorce, the boss from hell, the unexpected illness or the parking fine? Are you wincing yet? I winced too, when I first encountered this concept.

Weirdly, I first encountered the concept in a dance class. The teacher was playing the high-tempo track 'Everybody's

Free' by Rozalla. 'What are you grateful for?' he called over the music. 'What lights you up?' I thought about my son, my work, my home and my friends. I thought about my family and my dog and the joy dancing gave me. I thought about running through the woods and making heartfelt connections and I obviously thought about cake. I gave thanks for it all through my dance. My body tingled with gratitude. But then the teacher spoke again. 'Now dance gratitude for something or someone that's hurt you.' What the hell?! I closed my eyes and tried to stay focused. The first thing that popped into my mind was a guy I'd been working for who'd recently gone out of his way to belittle me in a meeting. The incident had been hurtful and demeaning, and I was still emotional smarting. How was I supposed to feel grateful for this? I wracked my brains as I danced. I thought back to the meeting – and how I'd stood my ground when my colleague had been so dismissive of my ideas. I suppose I could be grateful for the opportunity it gave me to be strong – even though inside I'd crumpled. I was genuinely grateful that I'd been tough enough to withstand the pressure and the humiliation. 'Give thanks now!' the dance teacher called. I raised my arms in the air and danced my thanks to the man who had pushed me to toughen up and forced me to stand strong. It only took a few seconds until I genuinely meant it. And this time the gratitude I felt was double strength because it came from a place of pain. 'Keep dancing your gratitude,' the teacher cried. I raised my arms even higher and gave thanks to Something More and *whoosh* – I felt plugged into the most incredible sensation of joy and peace. I'd danced the anger, hurt and fear from my body, and all that was left was Love.

Various scientific studies have shown the benefits of gratitude on a person's physical and mental health. In his article 'Sowing seeds of gratitude to cultivate wellbeing', spiritual author and teacher Deepak Chopra references clinical studies that have proven the benefits of a gratitude practice to patients recovering from heart failure. In his book *The Upward Spiral: Using Neuroscience to Reverse the Course of Depression*, Alex Korb talks about how gratitude boosts the feel-good neurotransmitters dopamine and serotonin and the hormone oxytocin. Gratitude is one of several areas where science and spirituality are converging, both showing that the rewards of a gratitude practice are life-changing.

Something More

Wonder walk

Take yourself on a 'wonder walk'. This would preferably be somewhere scenic but it doesn't have to be. There are opportunities for wonder on even the grimiest city streets – you might just have to look a bit closer to find them. As you walk, ask yourself what here makes you feel radically amazed. It could be a stunning landscape or a piece of architecture. It could be the giggle of a toddler or the wizened face of an old man – every wrinkle telling a story. It could be a wild flower somehow bursting its way through concrete. It could be the passing melody from a car stereo or the vibrant colour of the street artist's paint. Take pictures of everything that causes you wonder, or note them down in your journal, to imprint them in your heart and on your brain.

Shower of gratitude

I don't know about you, but I can often get ambushed by worry and fear first thing in the morning. The grogginess before that first cup of tea kicks in can be a killer. Here's a simple exercise to help get your day off to a positive start. While you're in the shower speak out loud a list of things you're grateful for. Speaking them out loud is much more effective than thinking them, and no one will hear you over the running water. I guarantee you'll come out feeling so much fresher, having washed away all of the worry and fear.

Daily gratitude list

This is the exercise that transformed my life after my marriage break-up. Every evening before you go to sleep, write down five things that you're grateful for. I'd like to add my own twist on this exercise and get you to also write *why* you're grateful for each thing. Really revel in the gratitude. Do this exercise every day for three weeks and I promise you'll start seeing the world differently.

From hateful to grateful

If you're feeling really brave – or really feel in need of a spiritual breakthrough – make sure at least one thing on your daily gratitude list is something that initially hurt or upset you. Seek out a reason to be thankful that it happened. Maybe it taught you a valuable lesson? Perhaps it toughened you up? Maybe you're grateful for the opportunity it brought you to love in spite of your pain.

Write thank-you letters

Spread your love to others and gratitude to them by writing them surprise thank-you letters, emails or texts – for no other reason than that you're thankful that they're a part of your life. Notice how writing and sending these messages makes you feel. When you give Love you instantly tap in to and receive Love. It's an important lesson to learn. Contrast it with how you feel when you spend time bitching or moaning about others. There's no comparison, right?

9

MANIFESTING ABUNDANCE . . . AND FALSE GURUS

Be content with what you have, rejoice in the way things are. When you realise there is nothing lacking, the whole world belongs to you.

Lao Tzu

In 2006, a film called *The Secret* was released, along with the kind of tsunami of hype that's a promoter's dream. A couple of days after it came out a friend of mine called me. 'I've got a copy of the DVD,' she said in hushed tones, as if she'd just discovered the Holy Grail itself in the film section at Woolworths. But I have to admit that I was excited too. According to the trailer, *The Secret* would give you everything you want in life. Literally, *everything*, and especially money, and who doesn't want that? The truth is, I had a long-held fear around money, or rather, not having enough money. It began when I was at university. Most of the students I knew came from affluent families; some had even been given credit cards by their parents so they'd never go short. I, on the other hand, grew up on a council estate and had no affluent family to fall back on. All I had was a student grant, whatever money I could earn during the summer holidays and an ever-increasing overdraft. Towards the end of my second year I can remember being so broke that I could only afford to eat toast for breakfast, lunch and dinner. I hated living like this. When I got a job in a video store during the summer holiday, I was so relieved that I was able to start paying off my debt that I decided to drop out of university.

By the time *The Secret* was released I wasn't working in a shop any more but was a self-employed, single mum, living with the bubbling fear that my son and I were just one unpaid invoice away from poverty. So I got a group of friends together and we all watched the film in eager anticipation. The opening footage consisted of a montage of slightly cheesy clips, showing 'The Secret' being passed down through history, from the Emerald Tablet to the Knights Templar, to the Catholic Church, finally cutting to the modern-day boardroom of a business elite. The atmosphere was ramped up by the mysterious and impossible to decipher whispers of an unseen woman. The implication was that the secret to everything had been hidden from everyone – until the release of this slightly naff DVD. This wasn't actually true. The secret the film referred to was the Law of Attraction, something that had begun life as the New Thought movement in America in the late nineteenth century. The New Thought movement held the following four core beliefs:

- God or universal intelligence is 'supreme, universal and everlasting'.

- All people are spiritual beings and divinity dwells within each of us.
- The highest spiritual principle is loving one another unconditionally.
- Our mental states manifest our reality.

It's this last core belief that Rhonda Byrne, the creator of *The Secret*, focused on, citing the New Thought book *The Science of Getting Rich* by Wallace Wattles as inspiration for the film. My friends and I watched as various business people and life-coach types talked about how they'd used the law of attraction to manifest wealth beyond their wildest dreams. Vision boards frequently featured along with the word 'vibration'. Attracting wealth, love and happiness was talked about as if it were a scientific law, using quantum physics to back it up.

In a nutshell, quantum physics explains the nature and behaviour of matter and energy on the atomic and subatomic level, concluding that ultimately everything in the universe is made up of energy. Let's take us humans as an example. At first glance it would appear that we're undeniably solid creatures, made up of skin, organs and bones. But when you start to break down our bodies, our skin, organs and bones are actually made up of cells, which in turn are made up of molecules, which are made up of atoms, which are made up of subatomic particles, which are made of pure energy. According to quantum physicists, this energy flashes in and out of being every millisecond. If you're struggling to get your head around this, and I certainly did, try thinking of films. They are made up of numerous separate frames, but because they play so quickly you see one continuous moving picture. Our eyes can't see the gaps between the shots, just as they can't see the energy pulsating away at the heart of everything, from supposedly solid objects to empty spaces and even our thoughts.

This is where the Law of Attraction comes in – if our thoughts are made up of the same energy as everything else in the universe, even material things, then they can attract material things to them because energy has magnetic properties. Energy also vibrates and our thoughts vibrate at different frequencies. Positive thoughts, such as *Life is wonderful*, are high frequency, and negative thoughts like *I want to kill my upstairs neighbour for playing Eastern European hip-hop full blast at three in the morning*, are distinctly low vibe. Apparently, in the vibrational world, like attracts like. Therefore, if you're able to visualise yourself as wealthy beyond your wildest dreams, you'll attract wealth beyond your wildest dreams. And if you think of yourself as poor, you'll forever be shopping at Poundland because negativity attracts negativity. The New Thought movement even went as far as to say that all physical illness is first created in the mind; a manifestation of negative thoughts or feelings.

Due to its New Thought roots, the Law of Attraction is still deeply entwined with spirituality. In the twentieth century an off-shoot of New Thought emerged, called Prosperity Theology. This is the belief among some Christians that faith, positive speech and financial donations will manifest wealth, health and happiness, not to mention the private jets and mansions of countless televangelists. In her book *Blessed: A History of the American Prosperity Gospel*, historian Kate Bowler writes that Prosperity Theory is basically a mash-up of the New Thought movement and the American gospel of 'pragmatism, individualism and upward mobility' or, more simply put, the American Dream. Followers of the Prosperity Gospel argue that Jesus himself was a proponent of the Law of Attraction, citing as proof quotes such as: 'Ask and it will be given to you; seek and you will find; knock and the door will be opened to you.' (Matthew 7:7–8), and 'Whatever you ask for in prayer, believe that you have received it and it will be yours.' (Mark 11:24).

One of the biggest-selling books on the subject of the Law of Attraction in recent years has been *Ask and it is Given* by Esther and Jerry Hicks. Right from the outset the spiritual implications of the book are apparent, with the title paraphrasing the Jesus quote. In the Preface Jerry Hicks talks about his own quest for Something More, or as he puts it, to know what 'It' is all about. He refers to this 'It' as the Non-Physical and talks about how it is almost impossible to express what 'It' is in words, although a select few have been able to do so. Hicks cites some of these people as Moses, Jesus, Joan of Arc ... and his wife Esther. Although Esther doesn't take full credit for this, she claims she is channelling the thoughts of a collective spiritual conscious-ness named Abraham. Basically, Abraham transmits blocks of thought to Esther, who translates them into words via her books and talks. When I first bought *Ask and it is Given* and read this I put the book straight back on my shelf, where it sat gathering dust for years.

But then, a few years later, when I set out on my spiritual quest, I started seeing references to the Law of Attraction and the power of manifestation everywhere, often linked to the buzz-word or hashtag 'abundance'. 'It's not wrong or non-spiritual to want to manifest wealth,' modern-day spiritual teachers like to say. 'Money is simply energy. There's more than enough to go around. The only thing stopping you from being rich is your low vibrational thinking.' Hmm ... to me this theory seems like the definition of a first-world luxury and I can't subscribe to the view that the millions of people living in abject poverty around the world have brought it upon themselves simply because they didn't create a 'high-vibe' vision board. I mean, seriously. But then a Facebook friend of mine started raving about a 'spiritual wealth' programme she was taking part in, led by some kind of self-proclaimed entrepreneur/spiritual guru. Although I didn't know the woman that well, I knew that she was highly intelligent – a scientist, no less – so I trusted her judgement and decided to go to a free seminar her guru guy was holding in London. I wasn't interested in manifesting millions but I did long to feel more financially secure.

I should have known something was up straight away when, upon walking down the street to the venue, I was greeted every couple of yards by a manically smiling twenty-something – one of the guru's 'helpers' – dressed in black and bouncing up and down excitedly. We were then ushered inside the venue, where we were made to wait in the lobby – and wait and wait – until finally the doors were opened. I've subsequently learnt that this is a deliberate ploy, frequently used at these types of event, designed to build anticipation.

Once we were all seated in the conference room and the shiny, bouncy people were stationed, slightly menacingly, along every wall – the guru made his entrance. It was the kind of entrance normally reserved for a rock god. To the pumping strains of Bon Jovi, he bounded on to the stage, clad in alligator shoes and a designer suit. A huge gold watch on his wrist glinted in the spot-light. There then followed hours and hours of the guru speaking with no break. His talk was a weird mash-up of motivational business speak, spiritual teachings and quantum physics. The upshot of it all was that we create our own destiny (and material wealth) via our energy – and if we're able to change our energy, oh, and spend five thousand pounds on his programme or one hundred pounds on one of his 'limited edition' books – then we would become rich beyond our wildest dreams. At regular intervals during the talk we were encouraged by the shiny, bouncy people lining the walls to yell: 'Whoop! Whoop!' or 'Fuck, yeah!' Apparently not doing so demonstrated just how chronically negative our energy was. I sat there with my arms folded and my mouth tightly shut, my dad's favourite mantra 'What a load of old bollocks' echoing around my head.

Just before they finally let us out for (very late) lunch, the guru got us to think of the person we loved most in the world. I instantly thought of my son.

'Now imagine your loved one coming back from the doctor and telling you they don't have long to live,' he said.

My head began to ache.

'But – there is an operation that will save them,' he continued. *Phew!*

'But it will cost five thousand pounds.'

How odd. Exactly the same amount as your bullshit programme.

'Would you be willing and able to find that money from somewhere?' he yelled.

'Whoop! Whoop!' cried the shiny, bouncy people. 'Fuck, yeah!'

'Yes, of course,' people began replying.

'Aha!' Guru guy gave a triumphant grin. 'So, if you can find thousands of pounds to spend saving a loved one, why can't you spend it on saving yourself?'

But it wouldn't be on saving myself, would it? I wanted to yell. And if I wasn't feeling so hot and dehydrated, I probably would have. *It would be on financing your next Ferrari or Rolex, you cheating piece of shit.*

Finally, they opened the doors for lunch and off I ran. One

huge cup of coffee and a slice of cake later, I started to feel a bit more human. Then I did a Google search for the guru – which admittedly I should have done in the first place – and found reports of him scamming people from all over the world. The thing that annoyed me the most about the whole experience was that he'd dared to link his blatant money-making scheme to spiritual teachers such as Buddha and Ghandi. As far as I'm concerned, if money is your God, then be upfront about it. Don't try and dress up your greed as some kind of spiritual work in the world.

As I trudged home that day I pondered the question, how *should* we approach the subject of abundance from a spiritual perspective? How can it be right or loving to crave material wealth for ourselves when so many people in the world are living in poverty? And if you do have some kind of magical manifest-ing powers, as so many of these gurus claim to have, why not use them to help some of the millions in dire need instead of lining your own pockets? Although I was no longer a Christian, I found myself wondering what Jesus would do. Circling back to the Jesus quote used in *Ask and it is Given*, there are numerous occasions in the Bible where Jesus makes it clear that he doesn't condone material greed – like in this quote from Luke 12:15: 'Be on your guard against all kinds of greed; life does not consist of an abundance of possessions.' And I think we're all familiar with what he said about the rich and camels and the eye of a needle. So why, then, did Jesus say that whatever people ask for in prayer will be given to them? If you look at the quote in con-text he immediately goes on to say that God will not fail to give his children '*good things*' in answer to their prayers (Matthew 7:11). Surely the inference here is that our prayers are answered with what God deems to be good – or, as I prefer to think of it, what Love deems to be good. Instead of sticking pictures of Ferraris on our vision boards, and visualising astronomical wealth to hoard to ourselves, shouldn't we be making the focus of our manifestations Love, pure and simple?

Buddhism and Hinduism are also often referred to in conjunction with the Law of Attraction, most specifically in relation to the concepts of karma and dharma. Karma is the belief that what we send out into the world, such as thoughts of happiness or hatred, will come back to us. Dharma means the cosmic law and order of all things. But, just as with Jesus's teachings, when you study the scriptures of Buddhism and Hinduism there's no mention of using cosmic laws to fill your bank account. In both Hinduism and Buddhism the ultimate goal is to reach a state of enlightenment and an end to suffering. A big part of this comes in the letting go of attachment to all things, rather than craving or acquiring more. Abundance is seen as a state of mind, a sense of fulfilment and inner peace.

Inspired by these spiritual teachings, I decided to go on a one-woman mission to see what would happen if I made the Law of Attraction and manifesting abundance all about spiritual, unconditional Love. Using the theory that you have to become what you want to attract, I made myself the starting point, trying to figure out ways in which I could embody Love. The first thing I did was incorporate a visualisation into my morning meditation, where I pictured Love pouring into me like a ray of golden sunlight. On the second day of my experiment, I remembered an exercise I'd once done in the cool-down section of a Biodanza class, where we sat with a partner and took it in turns to stroke each other's hands. The teacher had talked about how the body benefits from this kind of tender, loving touch; the kind of caress we so often give to our pets or kids but so rarely receive as adults. As I sat in meditation I stroked my hands. It was so nice that I moved on to stroking my hair and face, as if I was being a loving mother to myself. All of the tension in my body melted away, to be replaced by soothing love. The best thing about the exercise was that it was so simple, something I could do any time my stores of love felt depleted – like the self-love equivalent of charging my phone.

The next thing I changed was my inner voice. As I focused on loving myself I became acutely aware of how negative and unloving my inner voice could be, and for the first time ever I was able to stop it in its tracks. My simple self-love exercises made being mean to myself feel completely unnatural. Instead of calling myself a dickhead (my favourite self-insult of choice) for a plot hole I'd failed to see in the novel I was writing, I praised myself for my determination to put things right and do my best work. The difference this made was incredible, instantly lifting my mood from despondent to driven.

Another way in which I'd regularly been mean to myself – and I know I'm not alone in this – was over my appearance, instantly zooming in on my so-called flaws whenever I looked in the mirror. So I decided to start using an affirmation as a way of countering this, replacing self-criticism with words of love. I'd say this affirmation in my head at any time I felt a twinge of self-doubt, or whenever I was in a situation that required a confidence boost. Once again, the difference it made was instant and powerful, not just mentally but physically too. My posture was transformed. I walked taller. I held my head higher. I wasn't scared of being seen or of being loving towards others. I no longer felt I had anything to lose. The love I was filling myself with was strengthening me from the inside out, leaving no room for old fears or insecurities.

It wasn't long before my experiment began manifesting some very interesting outcomes. The first change happened in my work life. A few weeks before I'd begun my self-love quest, a French publisher had asked me if I'd like to write a young adult novel for them, inspired by the #MeToo movement. I was over the moon, as it's a subject I feel very passionate about – but then they made their offer and it was insanely low. To put it in context, it was less than the going rate for writing a children's picture book. To make matters worse, they wanted me to write the novel in just two months, as they wanted to cash in on the #MeToo movement while it was still popular. My initial reaction had been one of disappointment, but due to my passion for the cause I'd started writing the book. A week into my self-love experiment, however, everything changed. Everything changed because *I* had changed. I felt I was being taken advantage of and wasn't prepared to accept it. So I turned down the offer and started writing a novel for adults. This had been a long-held dream of mine but previously I'd been too scared to give it a go.

As an established young adult and children's author, writing a novel for adults would effectively mean starting from scratch, with no guarantee of a book deal. Spending months working on it would mean betting a lot that it would work out, something I hadn't been prepared to do – until now. For exactly the same reason that I'd turned down the book deal, this was down to my increased sense of self-worth. And here's the really interesting thing – although I'd just said no to a book advance, so I was financially worse off, the minute I started writing the novel for adults, I felt richer than I'd done in years because I was doing something I loved, and creating something with a message of love at its heart. (In fact, two months after turning down the

French deal, a UK publisher offered me five times more for the book.)

The second thing that happened involved some dirty dishes – trust me, spiritual lessons can come in the most unlikely forms. Full disclosure: I like a tidy house. I'm not obsessive about it or anything, but I do feel far more relaxed if my surroundings are clean and uncluttered, and a particular bugbear of mine is seeing dirty dishes left on the kitchen work surface. I feel the instant compulsion to wash them, but then I feel disgruntled that I'm the one always washing the dishes because other people haven't broken their necks to get to them before I do. One morning, about a week into my self-love experiment, I realised that I had a guest coming to stay but – shock horror! – I hadn't done the cleaning *and* there were dirty dishes in the kitchen.

Instead of berating myself for this appallingly slovenly behaviour I congratulated myself on the reason behind it – I'd been working very hard all week on my labour of love, my novel for adults. In this spirit of reckless abandon, I made myself a cup of tea and went back to bed. A couple of minutes later, I heard the sound of running water and the chink of crockery from the kitchen. My son had got up and *was washing my dishes of his own accord with zero prompting or nagging.* And then I had an epiphany. When you love yourself, you allow others to love you. I don't know if it's some kind of magnetic, energetic Law of Attraction thing, or just good old common sense, but the fact is that you need to give people the space to love you. Being a self-pity-filled martyr acts as a barrier, literally and energetically.

In the days and weeks following I saw more and more evidence that the more I loved myself, the more love I put out into the world – and the more I got back. One week, I randomly received a spate of messages from readers thanking me for one of my novels, and wanting to keep this flow of love and gratitude going, I spontaneously announced a pay-it-forward prize draw on my Instagram feed for three signed copies of the book. The winners nominated people as far afield as America, Australia and the Philippines. It was such a thrill taking those books to the post office and seeing the book love spread around the globe.

I started making a conscious effort to be more loving on my social media, posting things that I hoped would inspire, help or uplift others. Two women I'm friends with on Facebook but don't know very well in real life separately messaged me to ask if I'd like to go for a drink some time – both of them commented on the positive impact my recent social media posts had had on them. An actor friend I hadn't heard from in years got in touch after being inspired by one of my posts. He was performing in a play in Oxford and wondered if I'd like to come and see it as his guest. I loved the spontaneity of his request. We ended up having a brilliant weekend together, picnicking in the beautiful Oxford countryside, browsing around a market, and having heartfelt conversations about life and dreams. And it was made all the more magical when I thought of the chain of events that had led to it happening. The love I was manifesting inside me was coming back to me tenfold. My life felt truly abundant.

Something More

Loving touch

Sit comfortably and close your eyes. Gently stroke each of your hands in turn, as if you're caressing a beloved child or pet. After a minute or so, move your attention to your face. Lightly stroke your forehead, cheeks and the skin around your eyes. Move your fingertips down to your mouth and jaw. If you feel any tension in your scalp, stroke the top of your head and your hair too. Imagine you're being a loving parent to yourself. Observe how this simple loving touch makes you feel.

Loving thoughts

Become aware of the way you speak to yourself through your inner voice. If you're anything like the vast majority of the population, the chances are that your inner voice can get hypercritical. A good way of stopping it in its tracks is to ask yourself how you would speak to someone you loved in this situation. Practise saying the same things to yourself. Write down in your journal about how different being kind to yourself makes you feel, and note any positive outcomes.

Loving affirmations

Although I'd always thought affirmations were cheesy, there's definitely a method to their naffness. The fact is, if you've been living in state of fear or self-loathing and you want to be more loving, you need to rewire your brain. Repeating affirmations either in your head or out loud create new, more positive neural pathways. Create a loving statement about yourself. The affirmation I used for my experiment and still use today is: 'I am a beautiful being of love and light.' Repeat your affirmation in your head like a mantra any time you need a lift. Also repeat it when you're out and about. Notice any difference this makes to your physical being. Note any changes in your posture and your confidence levels. Do you feel more inclined to give love to others, now that you're giving it to yourself?

Pay it forward

Once you've increased the love inside yourself think about how you could pay it forward. This could be by doing anything from being more loving to the people in your life, figuring out ways to be more loving in your work, giving a random gift or doing a good deed for a stranger. Pay close attention to how paying it forward makes you feel. What do you get from it? See how manifesting, embodying and spreading love becomes a virtuous circle.

True abundance

If you're feeling a lack of abundance in your life, the first thing you need to do is root out any fear you might have around the subject of money. Try free-writing on the subject in your journal, using the following questions as prompts:

- What are you most afraid of when it comes to money?
- What would you do if your worst fear came true?
- Would it really be as bad as you imagine?

The last two questions are key because so often we don't take the time to properly examine our fears. Like a small child convinced that there's a monster living under the bed, we need to shine a light on the shadows in order to discover that the monster is really just a tangled heap of clothes. I used to tell myself that if my career dried up I'd end up homeless but this simply wasn't the case. When I took the time to really examine my worst fear I realised that even if I did lose my home, one of my friends or family members would definitely give me somewhere to stay – then I'd work my butt off to get back on my feet again.

Now, balance out the exercise by writing about your best-case scenario:

- What does living abundantly look like to you?
- In what ways is your life already abundant, remembering that there's way more to riches than money?

Once you've taken the sting out of your fears, do the Resting in Love meditation (see page 34) and ask the wisdom of Something More for guidance. Ask what the loving approach would be when it comes to your finances. Ask how you could be more loving to yourself when it comes to your thoughts around abundance and money. Then rest in love and trust that the answers will come. And when they do, free write about them in your journal. Brainstorm your way out of your fear.

10

TUNING IN TO TAROT

The true tarot is symbolism; it speaks no other language and offers no other sign.

A.E. WAITE

It wasn't until I was a couple of years into my quest for Something More that I came to realise how effective tarot can be as a spiritual tool. I'm certainly not alone. In the past few years there's been an explosion in the popularity of tarot, as it's been adopted by the spiritual but not religious community. You can now buy tarot decks in just about any theme, from steam punk to animal spirit to the divine feminine. But how exactly do you use tarot as a spiritual or divinatory tool and where did it all begin?

Tarot began for me back when I was a very young child. Every summer a fair would come to my home town for one day only. It was a major event in my childhood calendar, but unlike my friends, who were obsessed with the attractions of the fair, I was more intrigued by the people who worked on the fair – the tattooed men who manned the rides, fearlessly jumping into the paths of the dodgems, and the heavily made-up women behind the stalls, with their money pouches and ears full of gold rings. While my friends gasped in awe at the rides, I'd be more interested in the caravans parked behind them. It blew my mind that people actually lived and travelled with the fair from town to town. It all seemed so exciting. The person I was most intrigued by was Gipsy Rose Lee – 'Fortune teller to the stars and royalty', as the board outside her caravan proclaimed. While other kids gazed awestruck at the big wheel, I would gaze at her caravan, hoping for a tantalising glimpse of headscarf or hooped earring. 'I wonder how she tells people's fortunes?' I once asked one of my friends. 'With her crystal ball and tarot cards,' my friend replied authoritatively (she had an older sister called Sharon, who was a mine of information on just about everything).

I had no idea what tarot cards were but they only added to the mystery. Were they like greetings cards, but containing messages like 'You will marry a tall handsome stranger next Wednesday' instead of 'Happy birthday'? Then, as I grew older and watched certain horror films, tarot took on a more sinister meaning, as tools of the occult, used to communicate with evil spirits. One of the cards was even called the Devil, and another, Death. Tarot became something to be avoided and avoid it I did, until one day my best friend Tina told me she'd bought a pack and asked if I'd be her guinea pig for practice readings. Now, as far as I knew, Tina wasn't a closet Devil worshipper so I agreed. I was pleasantly surprised by my first reading. It turned out that the cards all had a specific message to convey, and that put together in a spread, their messages formed a story. Even the more sinister-sounding cards were nothing to worry about. It turned out that Death just symbolised the end of something and the Devil meant being seduced by material pleasures.

My first experience of tarot was so positive that I decided to invest in a pack for myself and do some investigating. It turns out that tarot dates back to the fifteenth century and was originally created for the simple – and distinctly non-occultish – purpose of playing games. These games were particularly popular in France and Italy. This shouldn't come as any surprise really, as tarot decks are actually very similar to ordinary playing cards, containing four different suits. However, instead of hearts, diamonds, clubs and spades, the tarot suits are Wands, Cups, Pentacles and Swords. Just as with traditional playing cards, each suit is numbered from Ace to Ten, and contains a King, Queen, Knight and Page. These four suits are referred to as the Minor Arcana. Tarot decks also include the Major Arcana, a suit of twenty-two additional cards, each representing a life situation or experience. Although each card of the Major Arcana is a stand-alone card, with its own unique wisdom and meaning, the order of the suit also tells a story. It begins with The Fool and charts his progress through the next twenty-one cards, as he learns life's valuable lessons, ultimately growing into a complete being, as symbolised by the final card – The World.

It wasn't until the eighteenth century that tarot cards began to be used for divinatory purposes. The word divination comes from the Latin *divinare* and means to be forseen by some kind of supernatural means. In a spiritual context, the supernatural would refer to whatever you take that mysterious Something More to be. When I use tarot cards, I tune in to the same loving presence that I do in meditation, the same loving wisdom I turn to in prayer. In a sense, using tarot spiritually is a form of prayer, as you're asking Something More to guide you to pick the cards you need to see, containing the messages and lessons you need to hear. When I shuffle my cards I say a quick prayer, asking for exactly this. Using tarot cards for this kind of spiritual guidance can be especially useful if you're going through a stressful or fearful time and can no longer see the wood for the trees. In effect, you're asking Love, the universe and your intuition for their help and guidance. Moreover, the joy of using tarot as a spiritual tool is that you can make it as simple or as detailed as you please. Here are a couple of ways in which I use tarot for divine inspiration.

SPIRITUAL THOUGHT FOR THE DAY

I often pull one tarot card in the morning, kind of like a spiritual thought for the day. When I did it this morning I got the Five of Pentacles. The first thing I do when I pull a card is look at the picture and use my intuition to lead me to certain details and study it for meaning. The Five of Pentacles shows a woman and man walking through a snowstorm. The woman is trudging, head down, and the man is on crutches and limping. A beautiful stained glass window glows next to them, containing five pentacles shining like huge golden coins. But the couple are so beaten down by the storm that they fail to see the beauty right by them.

Once I've studied the picture for meaning, I think of how it might apply to my life. When I woke up this morning I felt overwhelmed by the amount of work I have to do. I was like the woman pictured on the card, feeling beaten down by the storm. Drawing this card was a pertinent reminder that I have so much to enjoy in my life. By switching my focus to gratitude – that is, by appreciating the symbolism of the beautiful stained glass window in the card – my stress about work is instantly lifted.

PAST, PRESENT, FUTURE

Another simple spread I like to do is one I call 'Past, Present, Future', where I think about an issue I'm facing and pull three cards, once again praying to Something More for guidance. The first card I pull represents the recent past regarding the issue, the second how things are right now, and the third guidance for the future. Recently, I did this exercise, asking for guidance in my personal life. As I shuffled the cards I said this prayer: 'Please guide me in my personal life, please show me what I need to do to get to move into the best possible outcome.' I pulled the following cards:

Past – Five of Wands The card shows a group of men all holding large branches, in a scene of conflict and confusion. Although they don't appear to be fighting, they are getting in the way of each other, their branches crossing and clashing. The official meaning of the Five of Wands is scattered energy, and focusing on too many projects. When it comes to my personal life in the recent past, this definitely rings true. I've felt so caught up in so many different work projects that there hasn't seemed to be the time or energy for a romantic relationship.

Present – Ten of Pentacles The card shows a man and woman standing together, the woman gazing at the man. Around them are an old man, a child and a pair of dogs. A tower looms in the background and golden pentacles are all around. The thing that first strikes me about the card is the way in which the woman is looking at the man. Recently, and for the first time in ages, I've noticed a man. The official meaning of the card is a stable financial situation, reflecting rewards from past and present efforts – in summary, the good life. This sums up where I am right now. The hard work of the past few years has paid off and now I'm ready to turn my attention to matters of a more personal nature. But how should I move forward? I turn to the future card.

Future – Ace of Wands The card depicts a huge white hand holding a branch. The hand is illuminated, indicating some kind of higher power. Leaves are falling from the branch but some are staying. My attention is drawn to what looks like a castle on a hill in the background – could this symbolise a happy secure home? I take the hand shaking leaves from the branch to mean that I need to make space for a relationship, getting rid of the old to make way for the new, like autumn and winter making way for spring. The official meaning of the card is to take inspired action to achieve your goal. This is perfect advice for me, as I have a tendency to hang back and not take action when it comes to my personal life, expecting the right person to just rock up at my door.

Taken as a whole, this simple three-card reading has really helped me to see clearly where I've gone wrong in the past, how this has led to my present situation, and what I need to do to capitalise on recent breakthroughs and achieve a happy future.

A CAUTIONARY TAROT TALE

Although I'm a huge fan of using the tarot as a spiritual tool I'm also aware that there can be some serious pitfalls, especially if you want to read for others, or if you ask someone else to read for you. The fact that tarot is essentially a deck of playing cards means that it's a completely neutral tool. The cards themselves aren't imbued with any special magic powers – and neither is the person reading them. I can't stress this enough. I've seen friends who, when going through particularly vulnerable times in their lives, such as a relationship break-up, turn to a tarot reader for consolation. They want to be told that everything's going to be all right, and are in desperate need of meaning. If the person reading for them is coming at tarot from a spiritual point of view, then they will want nothing more than to help them. They will be aware that it's their client's intuition that leads them to choose the cards they draw. The reader will understand that they are there to simply convey the meaning of each card and look for the underlying story and theme of the spread. Problems only arise when tarot readers make it all about them. This is the flip side of the growing popularity and 'coolness' of tarot. There's a danger that some people might be drawn into reading the cards purely as an Instagram-friendly career option, hashtag ultra-spiritual.

I recently went to a Mind, Body and Spirit fair where various tarot readers were offering taster sessions. As I walked around the hall, all of the readers were busy apart from one woman. I asked if I could have a ten-minute taster and sat down at her table feeling open, upbeat and curious as to what advice she might give me. Ten minutes later I left feeling bewildered, drained and seriously angry. The first thing that felt slightly

off about the reading was that she set a timer. I've never had a
tarot reader do this before and it instantly made me think she
was a little mean-spirited. She was charging fifteen pounds for
ten minutes after all.

She then asked me to shuffle the cards, split them in three
and choose a pile. Once I'd done this, she began laying out the
cards and the reading began. Here are some highlights:

TAROT READER: You're Libran, aren't you?

ME: No

TAROT READER: Really? Got to be Cancer then?

ME: No.

TAROT READER: Sorry, I meant Pisces.

ME: (*realising there are a lot of signs in the zodiac*)
I'm Taurus.

TAROT READER: (*staring at me as if this is truly
unbelievable*) No way!

*There followed several other wildly inaccurate statements, all
of which were uttered with absolute certainty until:*

TAROT READER: (*pulling card*) You've suffered a lot from
depression in your life.

ME: No. I'm actually a very upbeat person.

TAROT READER: Oh. Are you feeling a bit down at
the moment?

ME: No!

TAROT READER: (*frowning*) Have you experienced the
death of someone close to you?

ME: What, ever?

TAROT READER: Yes.

M E: Well, yes.

T A R O T R E A D E R: That'll be it then. You're not over it yet.

M E: I think I am . . .

Tarot reader patronisingly shakes her head, before laying down another couple of cards.

T A R O T R E A D E R: Oh! you have two sons.

M E: No, just one.

T A R O T R E A D E R: Are you sure?

M E: (*wondering briefly if I once gave birth to a son so dull I forgot about his entire existence*) Yes, I'm sure.

T A R O T R E A D E R: Are you sure you don't have another son in spirit?

M E: No!

T A R O T R E A D E R: Are you sure?

M E: I think I'd remember if I'd lost a child.

Awkward silence, broken only by the sound of the tarot reader tapping her long, false fingernails on the card supposedly symbolising my second son.

T A R O T R E A D E R: Oh! It's not a second son, it's a lover. Yes, you're going to have a young lover. This summer. Isn't that nice?

Tarot reader's timer starts bleeping loudly.

Now, I'm aware that this would make a great comedy sketch but there is a serious message in this cautionary tale. I was in a really positive and strong frame of mind when I saw the tarot reader, and although she annoyed me, I was able to brush it off and ultimately laugh it off. I'm also familiar with the meanings of tarot cards and knew that some of her interpretations were completely wrong. But what if I'd been feeling vulnerable? What if I had no prior knowledge of tarot and had no idea what the cards meant? Her reading could have seriously shaken me. It seemed to be all about proving her right and me wrong – even when it came to how many children I had. It left me feeling seriously unsettled.

The moral of this sorry tale? If you're going to have your cards read by someone else try and go to someone who's been recommended to you. The fact is, anyone can set themselves up as a tarot reader and write a load of fake testimonials for their website. I know I might be coming across as very cynical here but tarot can be a very intimate business, especially if you're using it as a spiritual tool. When looking for a tarot reader I'd recommend doing the same due diligence that you would use when seeking the help of a counsellor.

Something More

Tarot is great for tuning in to the presence of Something More in your life and asking it for guidance. If you don't already own a tarot deck I'd recommend you start with the classic Rider-Waite deck as the images are great for finding inspiration. Try the following exercise to start with.

Asking for guidance

Give your cards a good shuffle, all the time thinking of an issue in your life you need some guidance with. Then cradle the deck in both hands, close your eyes and pray to whatever you take Something More to be that it leads you to the card you need to see. Once you've said the prayer, place the deck of cards in front of you and split it in two with your non-writing hand. Put what would have been the bottom pile on top of the other pile and turn over the top card.

Gaze at the picture and notice which details your eyes are drawn to. It could be the main image, or a smaller detail in the background or corner. Let it happen naturally. Once you've found the details you're particularly drawn to, ask yourself how they could be answering your question. In which ways could the card be advising you? Don't worry if you don't get anything at first or you feel unsure. The more you do this exercise, the easier you will find it to tune in. When you've gleaned all you can from the card, use a book or website to ascertain the official meaning of the card.

Write down your findings in your journal. Were there any parallels between your reading of the card and the official meaning? How can they help to give you guidance? How has the card answered your prayer?

Doing this simple exercise every day is a great way of getting to know the tarot deck and tuning in to your inner source of wisdom.

Reading for others

If you feel called to read for others as part of your spiritual practice, here are some things to bear in mind.

- Before your client arrives say a prayer out loud or in your head, tuning in to the presence of Something More and asking for guidance. Also ask this higher presence to work through you via your interpretation of the cards.
- See yourself as a channel for loving wisdom and make this clear to the person you're reading for too.
- Let your client know that a spiritual tarot reading is not about predicting the arrival of Mr Right on a set date, or any other kind of fortune telling. It's about tuning in to the client's situation and asking for guidance about where they've been, where they want to go and what they want to achieve.
- It can help to do a short-focus meditation with your client beforehand, to clear the space and both of your energies.
- Ask the client if there are any specific issues they need guidance on.
- Get them to think about these issues while they are shuffling and selecting their cards.

- Be ultra-sensitive to the feedback they're giving you at all times, both out loud and through their body language.
- Don't get caught up in the need to be right.
- Deliver all possible meanings attributed to the card so that the client can choose which ones feels right for them.
- Be on the lookout for recurring themes and the story of the spread.
- Try to link the themes together in conclusion so that your client is left with a clear and uplifting message to take away with them.
- Above all, focus on making this a loving experience.

11

YOGA, DEATH AND DOWNWARD DOGS

And you would watch with serenity
through the winters of your grief.

KHALIL GIBRAN

Great excitement hit our village when, one cold winter's day, leaflets began popping through front doors announcing the imminent arrival of 'a yoga instructor to the stars'. I was particularly excited, as yoga was something I'd tried a few years previously but following a mortifying incident, which can be summed up most concisely in the following equation: 'Beans for dinner + downward dog pose = me farting in the face of my teacher', I'd never gone back. Like many people in the West, I'd initially seen yoga as a form of keep-fit, but my growing interest in spirituality had taught me that it was so much more than this.

The word yoga first appeared some five thousand years

ago in the Indian sacred texts the *Rig Veda*, and referred to a group of physical, mental and spiritual practices. Yoga was then slowly refined and developed by the Vedic priests, the Brahmans. The most renowned of the Yogic scriptures is the Hindu text the *Upanishads*, composed around 500 BC. Then, in around the second century AD, a Hindu scholar named Patanjali organised the practice of yoga into an eight-fold path in his text, and one of the most important texts in the Hindu tradition, *The Yoga Sutras*. Patanjali is known today as the father of yoga. In his translation of *The Yoga Sutras*, revered yoga master Sri Swami Satchidananda writes: 'We are not going to change the world but we can change ourselves and feel free as birds. We can be serene even in the midst of calamities and, by our serenity, make others more tranquil.' I love the simplicity of this concept – that if we focus on the one thing in this world that we can control – our inner state – we can positively affect the outer state. Dance had taught me that moving my body could help me find inner peace and tune in to Something More, and now I was eager to try yoga again for the same reason.

The classes were taking place in the community centre at the end of my road. I set off for the first class unsure what to expect. The glowing celebrity endorsements on the leaflet led me to expect something slick and ultra-polished. What I got was in many ways the opposite of that, but so much better, because what I got was the real deal. Once everyone had arrived (there were about ten of us that first night), the yoga teacher, Ken, sat in the lotus position at the front of the class and introduced himself. He was wiry and tall with a mass of wild blond curls, and the fun and light energy of a child. In his lilting Irish accent he told us how, when he was a young man, he went to India and spent some time living alone in a tropical forest there. India had clearly had a profound effect on him and he'd subsequently spent a lot of time in the country, learning yoga from the masters.

Ken explained that when he taught yoga he wasn't interested in being critical and pushing people into so-called 'perfect' postures. He was more interested in gently encouraging people to open and relax into their true state of being. This was all music to my ears as one thing that had put me off yoga – apart from the farting downward dog incident – was the way it had been hijacked by the perfection police. I'd been left cold by the Instagram images of designer-clad women taking flawless selfies in flawless headstands, who were all #grateful and #blessed. If these women ever farted in downward dog pose I bet they only farted soft-focus rose petals. Ken, in his faded T-shirt and shorts, and with his unruly hair and classic Irishisms like, 'Sure, shall we do a few sun salutations, would that be a craic?' seemed to be the polar opposite of this.

In Ken's class I really started to see and, more importantly, *experience* the connection between the physical and the spiritual. The focus on breathing particularly helped with this. In every pose Ken would direct our breathing, telling us when to breathe in and when to breathe out and for how long. This had a hugely calming effect on my mind, quietening any inane chatter and enabling me to focus on the spiritual aspects of each pose. During the sun salutations – a foundational series of movements in yoga – I would focus on giving gratitude through my body. In the tree pose I would picture myself rooted and able to withstand the storms of life. In the child's pose I would allow my whole body to sink into the floor while my soul connected to Something More. During each class Ken would wander among us, gently encouraging us to go further into the pose and uttering quotes from spiritual teachings. There was only one pose that I really struggled with, which involved lying on my back with a yoga 'brick' beneath my chest. I hated how vulnerable this made me feel. Back when I'd just seen yoga as a form of keep-fit I'd have simply assumed that this was because my body wasn't used to being in this position. But now I wondered if there was something deeper going on here. Was the resistance I was feeling trying to show me something? Why did I find it so hard to open up my heart and my throat? Were my old barriers kicking in? With Ken's help I slowly but surely learnt to let go and open up without panicking. Overcoming my fear and opening my heart in a position that left me completely vulnerable felt strangely liberating. It was a powerful lesson in listening to my body and allowing it to teach and heal me.

Ken finished each class bowing with his hands in prayer position and saying 'Namaste'. Although I'd heard the word Namaste before I had no idea what it meant. So when I got home the night of the first class, I looked it up. It turns out that Namaste is a Sanskrit greeting used on the Indian subcontinent, and it literally means, 'I bow to you'. Another common interpretation of Namaste is 'The spirit in me honours the spirit in you'. The following morning, as I took Max for his walk, I thought about the significance of Namaste and realised that this honouring of the other person is a crucial step on the spiritual path. It's the 'Love your neighbour' that Jesus preached about, for once we realise that our true identity is Love, it follows that everyone else's true identity must be Love too. So when we see the potential for Love in others it feels natural to be more loving towards them – and if we're able to honour the spirit, or potential for Love in everyone, including those who hurt us, it makes forgiving our enemy that little bit easier. From that moment on I said Namaste with real meaning.

Another phrase that Ken was keen on was, 'I am that I am.' The first time he said it I was in a particularly ambitious pose and I have to admit it made me feel a little bit irritated – it can be hard being all Zen when you've got your legs wrapped around your neck and you're not sure you're going to be able to untangle yourself. *What the hell's that supposed to mean*, I thought as he kept repeating the phrase over and over. *You are WHAT that you are?* What I didn't realise at the time was that Ken was referring to a key spiritual teaching, which crops up in many different faiths. If I asked you what 'I am' means to you, the chances are that you'd reply with your name, occupation or relationship status: 'I am Kate,' 'I am a woman,' 'I am a wife,' 'I am a mum,' or 'I am a teacher,' for example. But the phrase 'I am' in a spiritual context needs no other qualifier. It refers to being itself, the consciousness that exists deep within us, beneath the masks our ego or personality create. The best way to understand this concept is to experience it. And the easiest way to experience it is in meditation.

When you sit in stillness it's possible to become aware of a part of you that is detached from all of the drama, fears, judgements and attachments that your ego is immersed in. There's a part of you that silently and serenely observes it all. This part of you isn't limited to your physical body – it feels completely and utterly limitless and without boundaries. It exists everywhere and within everything. The first time I experienced 'I am' in meditation it felt as if my entire body and personality had disappeared. Now, I wasn't just resting in Love, I was a part of it. In the Old Testament (Exodus 3:14) God appears to Moses and

Moses asks him his name. God replies, 'I am that I am.' Not 'Dave' or 'John' or even 'God'. Simply 'I am.' *God is being itself.* This makes perfect sense to me; that 'God' is the loving force creating and driving the universe and it exists inside everyone and everything. This would explain the shared experience of people of all faiths, and often no faith, who are able to tap into the feeling of being a part of something way bigger than themselves; who are able to experience that sensation of over-whelming freedom and peace. You don't need to be a member of a religion to experience this, you just have to *be*. This was a major breakthrough for me. I was learning so much more from Ken's classes than how to bend my body into weird and won-derful shapes. But the biggest and most painful lesson was yet to come ... when my dog Max died.

I'd never had a dog before I got Max. I'd actually got him for my son, thinking that as an only child, he'd enjoy the compan-ionship of a 'brother from a furry mother'. But it was clear from the moment that I collected Max from the rescue centre that he was my dog. He instantly attached himself to me like a shadow. It immediately became apparent that Max had been seriously mistreated by his previous owners. Although he was a big dog he cowered at the slightest sound, trembled if someone knocked at the door and worst of all, refused to leave the house. When I realised that I had the only dog in the UK – if not the world – who howled in fear rather than yelped for joy at the sound of 'Walkies!' I was distraught. Walking Max had been the thing I'd been looking forward to most about having a dog. I'd had no idea that he was badly traumatised and I had no idea what to do. That first night, after securing a howling Max in a room downstairs, as instructed by all the dog-advice websites, I got into bed and started to cry. My dog-owning dream had turned into a nightmare. I had no idea how to help Max. I'd have to send him back to the shelter. Then I heard footsteps padding across my bedroom floor – and felt something licking my face. Somehow Max had managed to escape from his room down-stairs and he was licking my tears away, as if to say, 'I'm sorry. Don't worry.' I knew there and then that I was in this for the long haul; that there was no way I'd be taking him back to the shelter in the morning. And so began Operation Rehabilitate Max – using the only two things I had at my disposal, love . . . and cocktail sausages.

Slowly but surely, we began to coax Max out of his shell and out of the house – with the help of the aforementioned sausages. It was a long and bumpy road to recovery, but the love I felt for Max was of the fiercest, purest kind. And it was a love that was more than reciprocated. Max was uncon-ditional love in four-legged form and it wasn't just me he showered his love upon. Back when I first got Max and I was still living in London I used to do one-to-one writing coach-ing sessions at my house. Occasionally these sessions would get emotional when I asked the writer to explore the fears holding them back. On one such an occasion a client started opening up about her deepest fears and she began to sob. Max, who always sat under the table chewing on a bone during my coaching sessions, emerged, went over to my client and placed his chewed-up bone on her lap. Now, to anyone else having a meltdown this might have been the straw – or bone – that broke the camel's back, but thankfully my client was a dog owner herself so she understood the huge act of selfless love that had just taken place. To Max, his skanky bone was his most treasured possession, but when he saw someone in dis-tress his first instinct was to give it to her. I truly believe that this is the kind of Love that Jesus preached about – pure and selfless and straight from the heart.

The thing I treasured most about Max's love – and another parallel with spiritual Love – was the feeling of constant companionship it gave me. Over the years, I walked miles with that dog, day after day, come rain or shine, literally and metaphorically. We walked together through good times and bad, and when the times got really bad, the one thing I could console myself with was the fact that we were still walking. My partner had cancer and might die – *but Max and I were still walking*. My son was having problems at school – *but Max and I were still walking*. My relationship had broken up – *but Max and I were still walking*. There was such safety and security in the consistency and companionship of our daily walks. So I was utterly devastated when the vet told me that Max had to be put to sleep. His back legs had become increasingly frail, he was in a lot of pain and he'd become incontinent. 'Having him put to sleep is the most loving thing to do,' the vet told me. It turns out that sometimes the most loving thing to do can be the most painful thing to do because sometimes loving means letting go. The day Max was due to be put to sleep I took him for one last walk around his favourite meadow. The sun was shining brightly and our shadows fell long upon the ground. My heart seemed to crack right in two as it hit me that from now on, his shadow would be gone. From now on, I'd be walking alone.

I don't really remember much about the journey to the vet but I'll never forget being there when Max was put to sleep. He lay on the floor with his head on my lap as I fed him treats and then, with a gentle sigh, he was gone. Although I was heartbroken I felt honoured to have been holding him when he passed away. It felt like the fitting end to our love story. But death is never the end when it comes to Love, and it took a yoga class to make me realise that.

Before the class began, I told Ken that my dog had died the previous day and I was still feeling very raw. 'So if I have to leave midway through it'll be because I'm feeling too upset to continue,' I explained. But once the class began, I felt a welcome respite from my sorrow. It wasn't until savasana that the floodgates opened. Savasana comes at the end of every yoga class and it basically involves lying very still on your mat in a state of complete and utter relaxation. It's my favourite yoga pose and I'm quite frankly an expert at it, but not that night. As soon as I lay down and put my blanket over me I felt my sorrow come flooding back with a vengeance. Although I was careful not to make a sound, tears began pouring down my face. Then I felt another blanket being gently placed on top of mine and tucked tightly around my body. The relief I felt was instantaneous and I felt a warmth rushing into me. I saw a vision of Max in his favourite meadow, but this time instead of limping in pain he was running free. And I felt awash with a tremendous feeling of peace – and a sense that Max was at peace – and this greatly comforted me.

When the class was over and the lights came back on I saw that Ken had covered me in an old woollen blanket. I took it back over to him and thanked him. 'The weirdest thing happened when you put the blanket on me,' I told him. 'I went from feeling completely heartbroken to the most amazing sensation of peace. It was as if my dog was telling me that he was OK and free from pain.'

Ken nodded and smiled sagely. 'That'll be the magic blanket,' he said. He went on to tell me that the blanket he'd wrapped me in had belonged to him since he lived in India.

'There's been a lot of meditating done on that blanket,' he said. 'And it's been sprinkled many a time with holy water from the Ganges.'

Later that evening Ken sent me an email which included the following words of wisdom: 'Love does not go away, one's capacity to love is eternal and self-perpetuating. Trust in the Love you feel and the sadness it now brings you ... Love heals the wounds it makes.'

Love heals the wounds it makes. Love hurts. But it also heals. The cycle is never-ending. The pain you feel after the loss of a loved one is in direct proportion to the joy they brought you while they were alive. And that joy and that Love will help you to heal again. It's been five years since Max passed away. I still feel pain at his loss – I cried while writing this chapter. But I still feel him with me too because Love can never die.

Something More

If you're a beginner to yoga try these simple poses as a great way of bringing your mind, body and spirit back into alignment.

Mountain pose

This is a great exercise for grounding yourself – a perfect way to recalibrate in times of stress, or at the beginning of a new day.

Stand with your feet together, arms down by your sides, hands facing inwards. Press all of your toes into the ground. Pull your kneecaps in and up. Do the same with your stomach, pulling your abdominals in. Open your chest and lower your shoulders, feeling the shoulder-blades coming together, keeping the palms of your hands facing in towards your body. Stand tall, imagining there's a thread drawing the top of your head up towards the ceiling. Breathe deeply from the diaphragm. Hold this position for five long, slow breaths.

Child's pose

This is a really simple pose, perfect for relaxation and stress relief.

Begin on all fours, then sit back on your heels and stretch your arms out on the floor in front of you, palms face down. Lower your forehead to the floor between your arms (it's fine to use a cushion or pillow to support your head if need be) and let your entire body relax. Stay in the pose for as long as you need.

I am meditation

The next time you do the Resting in Love meditation (see page 34) start repeating the mantra 'I am' silently, in time with your breath. So, when you breathe in, silently say 'I' and when you breathe out, silently say 'am'. As you repeat the words 'I am' slowly in your head visualise yourself becoming part of the golden sea of love on which you're resting, all boundaries dissolving. One by one, let go of all the identities you have – as a daughter, mother, partner or friend – and visualise them drifting away on the water. Let go of your name, your occupation, your age and your sex, until all that you have left is the essence of you, and all that you are doing is being, pure and simple. As always, if any thoughts come up, picture them like clouds high above you and watch them drift away too. Become the serene observer, totally at peace.

Afterwards, write down in your journal about how the meditation made you feel and any insights it gave you. The more regularly you repeat the mediation, the easier you will find it to detach from stressful situations. It truly is like being given a superpower.

12

DON'T REIKI AND DRIVE

Each and every being has an innate ability
to heal as a gift from the gods.

MIKAO USUIM, FOUNDER OF REIKI

Reiki is a form of energy healing that was developed by a Japanese monk called Mikao Usui at the beginning of the twentieth century. Translated, the word Reiki means 'universal life energy'. It is based on the belief that there is an energy or life force that flows through everyone and everything. This is not a new concept. In ancient India universal energy was referred to as *prana*. Native Americans call it the Great Spirit. In China it is referred to as *chi* (or *qi*). Chinese medicine and acupuncture are rooted in the concept of balancing and increasing this energy to promote optimal health. Reiki operates on similar principles. Its practitioners believe that when energy becomes blocked or imbalanced within a person's body, it can lead to physical and/or mental ill health. In their training Reiki healers undergo a process known as 'attunement', which enables them to work with the universal energy so that they can help heal energetic imbalances in others. There are three levels in Reiki training:

- Level 1 is the initiation into Reiki. The main focus is on opening the energy channels within the practitioner so that they're able to work with the universal energy. The emphasis at this level is on practising on yourself.
- In Reiki Level 2 the emphasis is on practising healing on others, both physically and remotely.
- Level 3 of the training process is to become a Reiki Master. This enables the practitioner to teach and attune others.

My first experience of Reiki was bizarre to say the least. When I was floundering in the emotional wilderness following the break-up of my marriage, a friend recommended that I go and see a Reiki practitioner she'd seen a few months earlier. So I found myself at a nondescript semi in the suburbs, with no idea what was about to happen and wondering how it had all come to this. It turned out that the house was far from nondescript on the inside. It was full of garish pictures and ornaments of angels, and from the carpet to the curtains to the toilet roll, very, very pink. The only thing that wasn't pink was the Reiki practitioner herself, who was clad from head to toe in a vibrant shade of violet. She showed me to a room upstairs and instructed me to lie on the treatment table. *This is just like coming for a massage*, I tried to reassure myself as I lay down, although no massage I'd ever experienced had involved crystals being placed all around me. The practitioner asked if I'd ever had Reiki before. When I said no she told me that she would be acting as a channel to heal any parts of my body that needed unblocking.

'Don't worry if you hear any sounds coming from me,' she said, somewhat disconcertingly. 'I'm just a channel. I won't actually be feeling anything.'

I shut my eyes and asked myself for the hundredth time why I'd thought this was a good idea. But then I felt the most intense warmth pouring into the sides of my head. It was coming from the Reiki healer's hands, even though she wasn't actually touching me. Her palms were a good couple of inches away from my scalp but the heat was intense. My body relaxed in an instant and within a couple of minutes I felt as blissed out as if I was having the world's best massage. I no longer stressed about what was going on or why I was there. My body sank into the table and my mind drifted and flitted, as if it were all a dream.

Slowly, the practitioner worked her way around my body, placing her hands over different points, which I'd later learn were my chakras – the key energy centres in the body. When she got to my throat I had a sudden flashback to a traumatic scene from my marriage and I heard her sniff. When she got to my heart the flashbacks intensified and she began to sob. Ordinarily, if someone started to cry in front of me my first instinct would be to ask if they were OK, especially if they were a complete stranger and I was lying prone on a table in their house. But I was in such a state of deep relaxation that I wasn't able to move a muscle. *She did warn me this might happen*, I reassured myself. *She's just being a channel for whatever's going on inside me.* Whatever was going on inside me seemed like a tragedy of epic proportions from the guttural sobs that were now echoing around the room. But I felt great. Even though I was reliving scenes that had been very painful at the time, it was with the detachment of an emotional tourist, viewing scenes from a stranger's life. When the treatment finished I felt more relaxed than I'd done in years but the Reiki practitioner looked wrecked. 'I was just a channel for your trapped pain,' she reassured me again, as she wiped the mascara streaks from her chin. Clearly there'd been a *lot* of trapped pain.

If you look up Reiki online you will find countless articles dismissing it as a 'pseudoscience'. In March 2009 the Committee on Doctrine of the United States Conference of Catholic Bishops, no less, declared Reiki a superstition incompatible with Christian teaching. Interestingly, there's a whole other school of thought arguing that when Jesus cured the sick he was using energy healing. Either way, all I knew was that when I had Reiki I had felt the energy pouring from the healer's hands into my body and there was no disputing the instant and powerful effect it had on me.

When I was a few years into my spiritual quest I decided to take the Reiki Level 1 training. An actor/director friend of mine called Stuart had recently completed all of the levels and become a Reiki Master, and he regularly raved about how much better Reiki made him feel. I need to point out here that of all my friends, Stuart owns the most impressively dry sense of humour and he most definitely doesn't suffer fools gladly. I take his opinions – be they on fashion, theatre or spiritual healing – very seriously. So when he offered to teach me Reiki Level 1 for free it felt like an offer I couldn't refuse. The notion of being able to 'heal' myself and others was very appealing, plus

I was intrigued to discover how you actually became attuned to work with universal energy. Normally, the attunement for Reiki Level 1 is done through four initiations over a period of two days but Stuart is a very busy man, so we did all four in his flat in an afternoon. Do *not* try this at home.

- The first initiation is designed to open your crown chakra (in the top of your head) to allow more energy to flow in.
- The second initiation opens your spinal column to improve the functioning of your nervous system, and opens your throat chakra to improve communication.
- The third initiation balances your left and right brain to promote clearer thinking.
- The fourth initiation focuses on your pineal and pituitary glands to raise your consciousness and improve intuition.

As far as I was concerned, Reiki attunement involved me lying down a lot while Stuart placed his hands over my chakras. Once again, I felt a tremendous rush of energy and warmth. Midway through the afternoon, Stuart showed me how to practise Reiki on him. As I placed my hands on either side of his head, I felt a tingling and heat like sun rays beaming from my palms. Stuart explained that when you practise Reiki on another person you have to look out for any changes in the tingling and warmth you feel in your hands as you move over the chakras. Any sudden increase in heat or tingling indicates some kind of imbalance and the need for healing, or as the creator of Reiki, Mikao Usui, put it, 'As running water smooths the jagged edges of a rock until it is small enough to roll away, Reiki flows to the areas of need, soothing and supporting the body's natural ability to heal itself.'

Stuart gave me a detailed manual, listing the different chakras and what an energetic imbalance in each area might represent. For example, sensing a blockage in the throat chakra could represent a problem with self-expression and communication. An imbalance in the solar plexus area represents fear, shame or anger. A blockage in the heart area shows signs of pain, sadness or isolation. Once a Reiki practitioner knows what each area represents, they are able to talk to their client about what they've felt, although no words are needed for the healing to take place.

With each initiation I felt increasingly relaxed, and by the end of the afternoon it was as if we'd been sitting around toking on high-grade cannabis for five hours. I remember very little about what happened and even less about my drive home – other than that at one point it felt as though my car was levitating. The moral of the story is: don't cram two days' worth of attunement into an afternoon. That night when I went to bed, I practised giving myself Reiki as instructed, moving my hands in a sequence over my head, eyes, throat, shoulders and hips. I dropped into a deep and peaceful sleep, and I've used this simple routine every night since. I didn't do any further training in Reiki. I didn't feel the desire to use it in any kind of professional capacity but it has come in very handy personally, working miracles on headaches and period cramps, not to mention insomnia. I would never recommend Reiki as an alternative to conventional treatments for illnesses, but as a method of pain and stress relief I've found it incredible. Science might not be able to prove the existence of a universal life force or energy, but that doesn't mean that it doesn't exist.

One thing I was learning on my spiritual journey was that the most magical things in life can't necessarily be proven by mathematic equations or scientific formulae, but they can definitely be proven by our own personal experience and that was enough for me.

Something More

You don't need to be attuned for Reiki to work on unblocking your energy. Thousands of years ago in ancient India spiritual teachers were recommending simple breathing techniques to help people do this. They called these techniques *pranayama*, with *prana* meaning 'life force' in Sanskrit and *ayama* meaning 'to extend' or draw out.

Breathing energy

Try this simple exercise to get your energy flowing.

- Sitting comfortably with your back straight, place a hand on your belly.
- Breathe in slowly through your nose, for a count of four, and feel your belly expand like a balloon.
- Then exhale slowly for a count of four, feeling your belly contract.
- Repeat this exercise for a couple of minutes, focusing on completely filling, then emptying your lungs.

Even if you're only able to repeat this breathing cycle a handful of times you'll notice the benefit immediately. It's a great way of calming down and increasing your energy. Best of all, you can do it anywhere without anyone even realising you are doing it.

Breath of fire

Breath of fire is a breathing exercise from the Kundalini yoga practice that involves rapidly breathing in and out through the nose. It is said to have many benefits, including the release of pent-up nerves or anxiety, strengthening the nervous system, helping the heart and circulation, and expanding lung capacity. It can be hard to do at first, so to start with only do breath of fire for about thirty seconds, increasing gradually to three minutes.

- Sit comfortably, with your back straight and your palms facing upright on your knees or in your lap.
- Take a few long, deep breaths from the diaphragm to get centred.
- Close your eyes and mouth and begin breathing rapidly and continuously in and out through the nose.
- There should be no pausing between the in-breaths and out-breaths, and they should be equal in duration.
- The breathing should be quite noisy and you're aiming for about two to three breaths per second.
- Make sure your stomach is expanding on the in-breath and contracting on the out-breath.

It's natural to feel a tingling sensation when you first practise breath of fire but if you experience any dizziness, take a break. It's also important to note that you should not practise breath of fire if you're pregnant or on the first two days of your period.

13

FINDING MY SHAMANIC ANIMAL GUIDE

We should know that the Great Spirit is within all things; the trees, the grasses, the rivers, the mountains and the four-legged and winged peoples.

BLACK ELK

One day, I was walking down the high street near the village where I lived and saw a sign outside the yoga studio saying: 'Shamanic workshop this Saturday. Come and find your spirit animal guide. Only £20!' If it had been more than twenty quid I probably wouldn't have gone, but my curiosity was piqued. All I knew about shamanism at this point was that it seemed to involve journeying deep into the jungle to take some weird cactus-based hallucinogen that makes you puke your guts up while discovering the true meaning of life – or something. The notion that I could do all this for twenty pounds on a British high street really tickled me, and I decided to try it.

There were about ten of us at the workshop, plus the shaman – a woman called Sandra from Hemel Hempstead. As we sat down on our mats my cynicism grew – especially when she told us that each of us has a 'spirit animal' to guide us through life and she was going to take us on a 'vision quest' to find it. I looked around the circle. Everyone looked pretty normal and no one else seemed to be fighting the urge to giggle. I decided to shake off my cynicism and see what happened.

Sandra the Shaman told us all to lie down on our mats and cover ourselves with the blankets provided. Then she lit a huge sage stick and wafted its incense around the room. The man next to me had a coughing fit. I bit my lip, yet again fighting the urge to laugh.

'In a moment I'm going to start drumming,' Sandra told us, her voice becoming deeper and slower. 'And then I'm going to lead you on your quest to find your spirit animal.'

I closed my eyes and focused on my breathing, certain that I wasn't about to meet any kind of spirit animal but wondering what it would be if I did. Instantly, I thought of Max. If there was any animal that I felt a natural affinity for it was my beloved dog. I bet he'd be my spirit guide – but only because I wanted him to be. I didn't believe for a second that an animal was going to show up from anywhere other than my mind.

'During the course of this meditation you're going to meet several animals,' Sandra went on, 'but you must wait until you've seen the same animal three times before you can ask if it's your guide.'

She began drumming on a round, hand-held drum – a fast, hypnotic rhythm – and I found myself beginning to relax. As she drummed harder and faster my body felt as if it was dissolving down through the floor. Guided by Sandra, I saw myself in a dark landscape. Within a few moments a dog came bounding up to me. *Aha!* I thought smugly, although it wasn't Max. *I knew it would be a dog.*

'You're trying to find your way down underground,' Sandra went on. 'See if you can find any kind of opening.'

The dog in my visualisation led me over to a bush. Behind the bush I found the entrance to a tunnel. I saw myself going down the tunnel and emerging in an underground landscape. I looked around and saw several different animals but there was no sign of the dog. Instead, a huge black horse came trotting over. I clambered on to the horse's back and flattened myself down, clinging tightly to his neck, terrified that I might fall off. The horse took me to an old abandoned house in the middle of a dark wilderness that wouldn't have seemed out of place in an apocalypse film. I dismounted and went inside. I felt as if I was looking for something but didn't know what. Then, when I tried to leave, I couldn't find a way out. I started to panic. What if I was stuck there? What if I could never escape? Then a deep, low male voice said, 'You created this house, you can uncreate it too.' I looked out of the window and saw the horse again, and knew that the words had come from him. I followed his advice and focused on 'uncreating' the house. In an instant it melted away and I got back on the horse, still holding on tightly but sitting a little more upright this time.

The drumming got louder and faster. The horse took me to the entrance of a cave. I went inside and saw a snake, a sheep and a fox. *Are any of you my spirit animal?* I wondered, but none of them responded. I carried on walking through the cave and emerged on the other side – to find the horse waiting for me. It was now the third time I'd seen him. 'Are you my spirit animal?' I asked.

The horse nodded his sleek head and told me to get back on. 'But this time stand,' he told me.

I stood on his bare back and he began to trot. Then his trot sped up to a gallop, but instead of feeling scared I felt elated. I flung my arms open wide and threw my head back. My hair billowed out behind me in the wind like a mane.

'If you've met your spirit animal ask them what wisdom they have for you,' Sandra's voice instructed from somewhere up above.

'What wisdom do you have for me?' I asked the horse.

'What can you see?' the horse asked, as he cantered even faster across the plain.

I looked all around me. From my vantage point standing on his back, I could see for miles. 'Everything!' I replied.

'Exactly,' the horse said. 'When you were afraid and cowering you couldn't see a thing, but now you're no longer afraid you see everything clearly.'

Now I was no longer afraid I saw everything clearly. And not only that, I felt wild and utterly free.

Sandra brought us back up from our guided meditation. A couple of people hadn't encountered a spirit animal at all but for the rest of us, the story was similar. We'd all met different animals, and animals we'd least expected – and they'd all imparted some great words of wisdom. The most powerful part of the exercise was that we hadn't just been told the wisdom, we'd *experienced* it. I'd never ridden a horse in my life before but every cell in my body was tingling as if I'd just completed a fearless bareback ride across a prairie. I hadn't just been told by the horse that I'd see things way more clearly when I let go of fear – I'd *experienced* it. I'd felt the relief when I realised that I'd created the fear I experienced when I thought I couldn't get out of the house and realised that I could uncreate it too. I'd felt the sweet freedom of letting go of fear and standing up on the horse. I'd experienced the sensation of being able to see for miles and miles once I'd let go. The whole experience felt like the perfect metaphor for all the times in my life when I'd been held back and blinded by fear.

When I got home I looked up shamanism and discovered a fascinating world of ancient wisdom. Shamans played a vital role in tribal societies all over the world, as doctors, shrinks, story tellers and philosophers – not to mention being pretty mean dancers and drummers. The shaman's drum is a sacred thing and shamans use the sound of the drumming to journey to 'other worlds'. Shamanic tradition is rooted in nature and helps us to tap into the power and wisdom that nature provides. I also discovered that in shamanism, the black horse represents awakening and discovering your own freedom and power. I bought myself a bracelet with a horse charm, which I wear every day to remind me of the freedom that comes from letting go of fear. I know that for many all this talk of talking animals will seem a tad far-fetched. For me, it helps to see what happened symbolically rather than literally. The guided visualisation the shaman took us on helped us access a deep inner wisdom. I believe it was the same inner wisdom that I had access to through meditation and prayer. The routes might be different but the destination is always the same – and available to everyone.

About a year later, at my writing group, I read the first draft of a chapter from this book, which I'd just started writing. Afterwards, one of the members of the group told me that I ought to meet a good friend of hers. 'She's a tarot reader and shaman,' she told me. 'And she sees clients in a caravan in her back garden.' This was such a wonderfully random combination that it was a suggestion I couldn't refuse, so I took down the shaman's contact details and made an appointment to go and see her. The shaman in the caravan was a no-nonsense woman with short, dark blonde hair and glasses. We sat at a small round table in her caravan, and she gave me a brief introduction to herself and her work. Then she told me about an ancient shamanic practice I might be interested in called soul retrieval. This operates on the premise that when we experience trauma or loss, part of our soul or essential self breaks away in order to survive the pain. This leaves us feeling disconnected and incomplete, which in turn can manifest as depression, anxiety and other, physical ailments.

In a soul-retrieval session the shaman will attempt to retrieve the lost parts of you and reintegrate them. I'd never heard of this before and just as with the journey to meet my spirit animal guide, I couldn't really imagine how it was going to work. But the shaman reassured me that I didn't really have to do anything other than lie on her treatment table and relax while she went on the 'journey' to retrieve the lost parts of my soul. So I did as I was told and lay down. The shaman began drumming . . . and drumming. I'm not sure how long it went on for, I drifted into a deep state of relaxation, then finally she told me to come and join her sitting at the table.

'I'm now going to tell you what I saw on my journey,' she said.

I sat back in my seat and nodded, still unsure of what to make of it all. As far as I was concerned she hadn't left this caravan in the heart of Sussex, but then I remembered my own shamanic journey to find my animal and how vivid it had been, in spite of the fact that I hadn't left my yoga mat.

'The first thing I saw was you as a teenage girl, curled up in your bed and crying,' the shaman told me. 'You were crying as if something had ended or someone had died. And the soul contract you made for yourself in that moment were the words, "I am not enough."'

I instantly had a flashback to the night before my parents' marriage officially ended. I'd thought about going through to my mum that night and begging her not to move out, but I'd come to the conclusion that it wouldn't work; that it – or rather I – wouldn't be enough. Of course, now I'm older and can be more rational and objective about it, I know that this wasn't the case. I know that my parents' divorce had nothing to do with me and how lovable I was, but as a child it's so hard not to take these things personally. I gulped and nodded, 'Go on.'

'Then I saw the part of your soul you let go of that day. She was a wild and carefree girl, sitting on a riverbank, swinging her legs over the water.' The shaman smiled warmly at the memory of what she saw. 'She was so carefree,' she repeated.

I felt a deep stab of recognition. This carefree part of me might have become disconnected but she's always been there in the background, peeping out from behind trees on my wood-land hikes and runs, cheering me on when I travel, whispering 'if only . . .' into my dreams. My parents' divorce forced me to grow up very quickly, and subsequently I've often felt burdened by a heavy sense of responsibility; a sense that I have to be strong and savvy, or else all hell will break loose. This strength has stood me in very good stead in life, but over the years I'd felt a growing yearning; a gnawing feeling that it had come at a high price.

'The next thing I saw was what your gift would be if you reconnected with this lost part of yourself,' the shaman continued. 'It was the image of a large, happy group of people, eating, drinking, chatting and laughing around a table – like an Italian family.' A shiver ran up my spine. This scenario has always been my definition of happy.

'Would you like to reconnect with this lost part of your soul?' the shaman asked.

I nodded enthusiastically.

She then performed a ritual involving stones, each of which symbolised the different parts of the journey. I let go of the stone that signified my belief that 'I am not enough', and reclaimed the stone that symbolised the lost wild and carefree part of me. Then the shaman helped me to create a new, more positive soul contract, an inner belief that *I am more than enough.*

The shaman asked me to lie back down, while she rattled and drummed and burnt a lot of sage and did other 'shaman stuff' and I basically chilled out.

I returned home feeling light and happy.

A couple of hours later – while I was cleaning the dishes, bizarrely – a picture of the wild and carefree person I could have been popped into my head and I burst into tears. However, unlike the tears I shed that night before my parents split up, these tears felt cleansing. They were the kind of tears you shed when greeting a long-lost, much-loved friend.

Something More

Retrieving the lost parts of you...

Think back to a time of pain or trauma in your own life. Do you get the sense that a part of you became disconnected as a result of what you went through? Have you subsequently experienced wistful moments when you've sensed this part of yourself trying to get your attention or itching to reconnect? Is there a braver, bolder, wilder, sexier part of you that was put to sleep by fear? Would you like to reconnect with this part of your authentic self? Once you've identified the missing part of you, ask yourself what changes you could make to allow him or her to reconnect with you. If it helps, free write about it in your journal, using these prompts:

- A painful and traumatic time for me was...
- As a way of protecting myself from the pain I stopped...
- A limiting belief I developed then was...
- The part of myself that became disconnected was...
- I sense that part of myself sometimes when...
- I could reclaim that part of myself by...

The most ironic thing about disconnecting from a part of ourselves to protect us from pain is that it doesn't work. Repression leads to frustration and depression. Here's to finding the courage to live life as our true and complete selves.

14

GOING ON RETREAT

*Let love read your soul, make it a place to
retire to, a kind of monastery cave, a retreat
for the deepest core of your being.*

ATTAR OF NISHAPUR

Spiritual retreats play an integral role in all of the major
world religions, albeit with slightly different intentions.
In Buddhism, retreats are seen as a time for reflection,
prayer and meditation. In Christianity, retreats are a way of
escaping the distractions of your day-to-day life in order to
reconnect with God – the practice dates back to the earliest
days of the Church, with Jesus's forty days in the desert used
as inspiration. The Sufi term for retreat is *khalwa*, which is
Arabic for seclusion but in the context of a retreat means
the act of total self-abandonment in order to experience the
presence of the divine. In recent years there's been a surge in

the popularity of non-religious meditation and yoga retreats, as an antidote to the stress and fast pace of the modern-day digital world.

It was the stress of the modern-day digital world that led to me going on my first retreat. Several years into my quest for Something More I found myself inadvertently caught up in that oh, so modern of woes known as 'The Twitter Shit Storm'. The experience left me feeling frazzled and disillusioned and, most importantly, disconnected from the source of peace and wisdom I'd come to enjoy. Thankfully, a guardian angel in the form of my friend Jenny came to my rescue.

Jenny is one of the most colourful characters I've had the pleasure of knowing. Tall and striking-looking, with a Cleopatra bob and commanding, theatrical voice, she's in her seventies but eternally young at heart. Over the course of her lifetime she has worked as an au pair, dancer, counsellor, astrologer and numerologist, to name but a few. Life is never dull when Jenny's around so, when I was at my disconnected, frazzled ebb and she invited me to go to a retreat in Spain with her, I jumped at the chance. Jenny had been a regular visitor to the retreat and in the years I'd known her she'd often regaled me with tales of her adventures there.

The retreat was in the foothills of the Sierra Nevada in the Granada region of Spain. I'd never been to Spain before so I had no idea what to expect. The drive from the airport was beautiful, the ocean glimmering in the sunshine on one side of the winding road and craggy, dark green mountains on the other. All the way there I kept thinking, *This is sacred country* – it all felt so epic and unspoilt. I could just imagine a giant hand of creation carving the huge ranges of rock, one huge finger pulling through the middle to form the valley. Then we started winding our way up the mountainside and the view became ever more breathtaking, with huge, snow-capped mountains looming in the distance like white-haired elders.

The retreat itself was a former farmhouse situated in an 800-year-old olive grove, surrounded by mountains. The region was once ruled by the Moors, who believed it was the paradise promised to them by Allah. I could see why. As I explored the grounds of the retreat I couldn't get over the beauty: the faded green of the thick grass, studded with black olives; the ancient trunks of the trees, so gnarled that they looked like characters from fairytales; the splashes of vibrant colour in the orchard. I'd never seen oranges hanging from trees before, and it was magical. There were about twenty of us on the retreat. The first night we ate together in the old farmhouse. The food was all locally sourced, fresh and vegetarian, and served buffet style by the local Spanish women who worked in the kitchen. It was delicious. After dinner some of us gathered in the living room around the fire for a slightly awkward, getting to know one another chat. Then we retired to our rooms for the night. The rooms were arranged around courtyards that burst with vibrant splashes of colour in the form of tropical flowers and palm trees. There were no TVs and no internet access. As I lay in bed hearing the wind rushing through the valley and the leaves of the palm trees it was like listening to a lullaby. My mind began unknotting and the stress of the previous months started leaving my body. I closed my eyes and said a silent prayer to the Something More I'd felt in the mountains, asking if it would help me rediscover my sense of joy and purpose.

As part of the retreat we all came together as a group each morning to have a session with a woman called Star. Going by her name alone, I'd imagined a young blonde from California, all big teeth and talk of hashtag lifegoals. I couldn't have been more wrong. There's a famous Buddhist saying: 'When the student is ready, the teacher shall appear.' Star turned out to be the perfect teacher for me at that point in my life – a true case of divine timing. She was from Manchester in the UK originally, but years previously she'd fallen in love with the retreat and now lived with about six dogs in a nearby house in the valley. She had long, silver-grey hair and a very calming, grounded presence, helped by her no-nonsense, northern accent. We gathered together in a large room with a huge fireplace and Star asked us to think about our 'growing edge' – the area of our life in which we were growing, and quite possibly experiencing some growing pains. The thought that instantly came to me was my role as a mum. My son had just turned eighteen and in a few months would be off to university. For so long it had been the two of us, but he was becoming an adult and needed to start making his own way in the world. My 'growing edge' was learning how to parent an adult son.

Once we'd all identified an area in our lives we needed some help with, Star told us to go outside and have a wander around the grounds and ask Mother Nature for her advice. I glanced at the other members of the group to see if anyone else was confused by this, but they were all nodding as if they under-stood her perfectly. I followed them outside and made my way down to a walled garden. Once there, I was instantly drawn to a stooped old olive tree. Its gnarled roots stretched across the ground like a pair of welcoming arms. I sat between them and leant against the trunk. I still didn't have clue how I was sup-posed to get advice regarding my issue from Mother Nature. It was hardly as if I could ask the tree how to parent an adult son – where was some cacao when I needed it? I leant back and closed my eyes, the gentle warmth of the sun kissing my skin. I felt so safe and protected, nestled there against the tree. I didn't need to say or do anything, but just relaxed, safe in the knowledge that it was supporting me. Then I had a light-bulb moment – Mother Nature had answered me!

To parent an adult I had to be like this tree. I had to be strong and rooted, and always there for my son, but supporting him from behind rather than engaging in the more in-your-face parenting you do when your child is young. I could no longer be so involved in the minutiae of his life. I had to give him the room to grow. I sat there in wonder at this silent lesson I'd been given and started to see the power of going on retreat. Away from the constant pinging of emails and texts, and flicking through tabs on a screen, there was the space and peace to access the true wisdom all around me.

Later that evening our group reconvened and Star asked us to think of what we wanted to achieve from our week on retreat, and the questions we needed to ask in order to get there. In the end, I came up with two questions. The first was to help me rejuvenate my love of writing and it was 'Where is the wonder?' The second was to help me spiritually and it was to ask 'Where is the Love?' in every situation. Then Star asked us to go over to an assortment of stones and crystals she'd laid out on a blanket in front of the fire and choose the one we felt most drawn to. I went straight for something big and shiny, which I'd thought was a crystal but turned out to be a large conch shell.

'How could you link the object you've chosen to your question?' Star asked.

As I turned over the shell in my hand I instantly knew. When I was a little kid my mum had given me a shell like this and told me that if I held it to my ear I'd be able to hear the ocean it came from. As I'd pressed the shell to my ear I'd been overcome with wonder at the sound of the rushing waves. Of course, I'd subsequently learnt that this is actually to do with the blood flow in your ears or something, but I'll never forget the feeling of wonder I experienced as a child. The shell was the perfect talisman to remind me to look for the wonder when it came to my work. That night I curled up in bed with the shell and my notebook and pen, and scribbled down the first ideas for a new novel. Once again, free from the constant noise of the online world, there was room for wisdom and imagination to come in.

The next morning, after a delicious breakfast of freshly baked bread, cheese and tomatoes just picked from the garden, we gathered in the meeting room and Star read us some poetry. A poem that really resonated with me was one by the Austrian novelist and poet Rainier Maria Rilke, titled 'Go to the Limits of Your Longing'. The title alone stopped me in my tracks. For the past few months I'd been fighting everything that had happened to me, internally at least, plagued by anger and resentment. The notion of just relaxing and letting everything happen to me was instantly soothing and the poem itself brought tears to my eyes. In the poem, Rilke talks about letting everything happen to you, good and bad. Nothing is final, everything is changing. I was emerging from the dark tunnel I'd been in for the past couple of months, making my way back to the light.

I loved the notion of God – or a loving presence – walking silently with us, holding our hand through the seriousness of life. The words 'just keep going' kept flashing through my mind. Nothing is final, everything is changing. I was emerging from the dark tunnel I'd been in for the past couple of months, making my way back to the light.

That night I woke up at about four o'clock. I grabbed the

thick woollen blanket from my bed and made my way up the stairs that led to the flat, terracotta-tiled roof. On one side of the sky the moon was shining brightly. The other side was completely dark. I sat cross-legged, wrapped in the blanket, staring at the darkness and waiting for the sunrise. All around me were the jagged black silhouettes of the mountains. In the peace and tranquillity I was able to slip into the serenity of 'I am' – the neutral observer inside. I drank in the mountains' power with each in-breath and exhaled my way deeper into the peace and stillness. Slowly, the sky on the horizon turned from black to inky blue, then violet, orange and pink. A new day was dawning – both literally and metaphorically.

As the week went on it felt as if my body was turning from solid to liquid, all of the tension slowly dissolving. I'd begin each day in the meditation room, a beautiful circular sun house at the end of the orchard. I'd light some incense, ring the resting bell (a small metal bowl that sounds like a gong) and let my breathing guide me into stillness. Then I'd meet the others for breakfast before our first session of the day with Star. The afternoons were free for us to do as we liked – chill out in the grounds or pool, take a stroll into the nearby town or go on one of the trips organised by the retreat.

Towards the end of the week we all strolled into the nearest town. It was market day, which meant that the place was a people-watching paradise. It turned out that there was some kind of hippy commune nearby, so the narrow, cobbled streets were full of deeply tanned people with dreadlocks in tie-dyed cheesecloth, mingling with the Spanish locals. Jenny and I browsed around the market. I bought a little figurine of Jesus for my dad and a necklace made from the wood of an olive tree for myself to remind me of nature's wisdom. Then, to our surprise, we discovered a Sufi cafe. It turned out that the town was home to the largest Sufi community in Spain, only adding to its magical melting pot quality. Jenny and I ordered fresh mint tea, which came in ornate silver pots, and we sat outside and watched the world go by. We enjoyed it so much that we decided to stay for lunch and moved to a table inside. The place had a really Moroccan feel, with vibrant wall hangings, velvet cushions and mosaic-patterned lamps. There was also a bookshelf, which I instantly gravitated to. I took down a book called *The Way of the Sufi* and had a quick flick through it. My eyes fell on a quote from a Sufi named Attar of Nishapur, who had apparently been a great inspiration to Rumi: 'The true lover finds the light only if, like the candle, he is his own fuel, consuming himself.' The book was crammed with inspirational nuggets like this. I took a photo of it on my phone, to remind myself to buy a copy when I got home.

The final lesson I was to learn from the retreat came on the very last night we were there. We'd all gathered with Star in the meeting room and a roaring fire was burning in the hearth. Star invited us to write down our fears on a piece of paper before releasing them to the flames. She also advised that we read them to the rest of the group before burning them so that we could witness each other's intentions. If this had happened at the beginning of the week I'd have been way too self-conscious to share my fears out loud, but by now we'd all well and truly bonded.

'I release the fear that I'll never find a partner,' I said, as I flung my piece of paper into the fire, feeling only ever so slightly mortified. Once we'd all released our fears and were getting ready to go, one of our group, a retired doctor, came over to me and placed a folded piece of paper in my hands.

'Just something I felt compelled to write to you after hearing you speak,' he said.

When I got back to my room I unfolded the paper and read: 'A message from across the gap of age and gender. Consider this . . . instead of seeking, why not wait confidently for the one who deserves you to find you.' How much wisdom is packed into those words? It was the perfect reminder that I had all the Love I needed; that I didn't need to seek and could wait confidently. It's because it is so much easier for the one who deserves you to find you when you let Love light you up from the inside, like the candle metaphor I'd read in the Sufi book the day before. Clearly this was a lesson the universe wanted me to learn; it seemed to be coming at me from all angles.

I returned home happier and more relaxed than I'd felt in a long time, if not ever. I was desperate to see my dad and tell him all I'd seen and learnt. We met the day after I got back and as we sat down at the pub table, he passed me a bag. Inside was a bar of my favourite chocolate and a copy of *The Way of the Sufi*. While I'd been reading it in the cafe halfway up a mountain in Spain, my dad had bought it for me in a bookshop in London. When the student is ready, the teacher shall appear – in all shapes and guises it seems.

Something More

Ask Mother Nature

Do you have a 'growing edge' in your life? A problem or issue that you need some guidance with? When you have some time to spare take yourself and your journal outside somewhere scenic and walk or sit with the intention of asking Mother Nature for her advice. Drink in your surroundings and listen to your intuition. Let yourself be drawn to the place you need to be. Then sit or stand silently and wait for inspiration. Pay attention to all of your senses. What do you hear, smell, taste, feel as well as see? Is nature providing you with any kind of lesson or analogy? How could you apply what you are witnessing in nature to the issue that's on your mind? Free write ideas in your journal. If no ideas come, keep walking or sitting until you find the answer you're seeking.

Create your own retreat

If you can't afford to go on an organised retreat try creating one of your own. Find a day, half-day or even an hour when you won't be interrupted, and switch off your phone and other devices. Use this precious time and space to sit in meditation, write in your journal, pray or walk in nature, with the aim of connecting to the strength and wisdom of Something More. Try using silence to deepen your retreat experience. If any feelings of discomfort or unease come up just be with them, witness them and allow them to pass. We can become so addicted to our phones that we literally need to detox from them. But the joy and peace you get from a solid chunk of time disconnected from the online world is a gift well worth detoxing for.

15

PILGRIMAGES TO THIN PLACES

*Heaven and earth are only three feet apart but
in thin places that distance is even shorter.*

ANCIENT CELTIC SAYING

The word pilgrimage is defined as 'a journey made to a sacred space as an act of religious devotion'. All of the world's major faiths have sacred places their followers make pilgrimages to. In Buddhism, various locations linked to the Buddha, such as his birthplace, Lumbini in Nepal, are popular destinations. Many Christians go on pilgrimage to Rome and other sites linked to the apostles, martyrs and saints, such as The Way of St James or Camino de Santiago in Spain. Hindu pilgrimage sites tend to be locations associated with their gods and goddesses. In the annual Kanwar Yatra, millions of devotees of the god Shiva travel to the River Ganges to gather sacred water. The Hajj, a pilgrimage to Mecca, is one of the five pillars of Islam and is seen as something every adult Muslim should do at least once in their life, if they are able. But what if you don't belong to a religious faith? Can the spiritual but not religious also go on a pilgrimage? The answer is, of course, yes, and I discovered how on my Spanish retreat.

Midway through the week, one of the retreat's organisers invited us to join her on a hike along an ancient medieval trail through the mountains. Before we began she recommended that we spend the time in contemplation, using the meditative power of walking to help us go within. Hundreds of years ago, when the region had belonged to the Moors, merchants would have travelled this trail with their donkeys, bringing fish and other goods from the sea to the remote mountain-side villages. Although we weren't walking *to* a sacred place, as is the tradition on pilgrimage, it didn't really matter as the whole place was steeped in spirituality. At one point the valleys would have echoed with the call to prayer from the mosques, and now the roadsides were dotted with Catholic chapels and shrines.

The shrines were beside the fountains that brought fresh spring water down from the mountains. They varied from kitsch displays of plastic flowers and figurines of the Virgin Mary, to a simple jam jar containing a cluster of bright orange marigolds. In one village there was a tiny chapel not much bigger than a phone booth. Sadly, it was locked, but I managed to peep in through a crack in the window. The interior was a riot of colour, with figurines of monks and angels, and a wooden crucifix festooned with pink plastic roses. As I was bombarded with these colourful declarations of gratitude it was impossible not to feel thankful myself. I felt so grateful for the beautiful sights surrounding me and, free from the distractions of conversation or my mobile phone, I felt present in the moment, at one with nature and completely at peace.

We followed the uneven and at times treacherous track through villages and fields, passing horses, hens and alleys full of cats. We also found orchards of orange, lemon and almond trees, the farmers tending the crops as rugged and wild as their surroundings. After hours on the rocky trail we joined a mountainside road where we didn't see a single car, just a succession of elderly locals out for an afternoon stroll, some of them still in their slippers. It occurred to me that pilgrimage might be more to do with state of mind than circumstances; that we all, at any time, have the ability to journey into a sacred peace.

We finished our trek at a bar on the mountainside. Mellow jazz drifted from the speakers as we sipped our ice-cold drinks. As I took in the stunning view I remembered a church service I'd been to where the man giving the sermon had said that God had created two Bibles – the written Bible and the Bible of the natural world. For me, the written Bible felt all too human, but as I closed my eyes and breathed in the fresh air and listened to the birds, I felt I had the only Bible I needed, there in the awesome strength of the mountains, the sparkling stream and the soothing serenade of the birdsong. Thanks to Star's words of wisdom, I was also seeing how 'God' offered us countless lessons in the natural world, if only we opened our eyes to them. I thought back to our trek and the lesson the rocky trail had taught me: when the going gets tough, all we can do is focus on taking the very next step. But if we keep on doing that, staying perfectly focused in the moment and not trying to skip ahead or look behind, we'll get where we need to be safely.

A couple of days later we went on another pilgrimage, this time to a Tibetan Buddhist monastery high up in the mountains. The monastery was called Osel Ling, meaning 'clear light'. As soon as we arrived we were greeted by a hand-painted sign saying '*Silencio*'. And the silence was so thick that it felt as if you could slice it. There were no monks to be found, so our group began making our way up the mountainside. As soon as we got to the first temple area I felt a powerful opening sensation in my chest and the most incredible feeling of peace washed through me. The ancient Celts believed that, in certain places, the distance between heaven and earth disappears and you're able to experience divinity. They called these 'thin places'. Osel Ling is definitely one of these places, in my experience at least.

Above our heads frayed rectangles of fabric in faded shades of red, white, yellow, blue and green were threaded on pieces of string and flapped wildly in the wind. They looked stunning against the vivid blue of the sky. Jenny explained to me that they were Tibetan prayer flags and each of the colours represented one of the five elements. As I looked closer I saw that the flags were covered in faded black symbols and writing. These were prayers and mantras designed to promote peace, strength, kindness and wisdom. The Tibetans hang their prayers like this so they'll be blown on the wind to benefit all of humanity. I loved this notion and took a moment to imagine the love woven into the faded, frayed fabric being blown out across the valley, over the mountains and sea.

We carried on climbing to the various shrines and temples dotted on the mountainside. As I climbed I said a silent prayer that the peace I'd felt when we first arrived would grow. But then one of the women in our group started to panic. It turned out that heights weren't really her thing – and neither were rocky mountain trails as she had a dodgy knee. She didn't want to wait for us on her own, so I offered to help her. As she clung to my arm and started moaning loudly about how much she hated heights and how her 'bloody knee was giving her gyp', I couldn't help feeling a little resentful. I'd never been to a place as tranquil as this but now, instead of sinking into the silence and opening myself up to some kind of profound spiritual epiphany, I was having to listen to a litany of complaints about mountain trails and knee replacements. Almost instantly I heard the wisdom of Something More inside my head: *If helping someone up a mountain isn't a spiritual opportunity, I don't know what is!* Humbled, I quit my inner moaning and focused on cheering up the woman instead. On Canterbury Cathedral's Pilgrim's Way website they advise that an important part of being a pilgrim is being open to help one another: 'Learning to be adaptable is the mark of a real pilgrim. It's when the best things often happen.' I was soon to learn how true this is.

Finally, we made it to the top of the mountain and a beautiful water feature, with a statue of Green Tara seated in the centre. Tara pops up in various guises across different strands of Buddhism and Hinduism. Some people view her as a goddess and others as a female Buddha. The Tibetan branch of Vajrayana Buddhism views Tara as a bodhisattva (an enlightened being) representing compassion and action. Tara also comes in different colours, most commonly green and white. The statue at the Tibetan monastery was a beautiful shade of jade green. Green Tara is believed to offer protection from fear, pride, ignorance, anger, jealousy, wrong views, avarice, attachment and deluded doubts. As I sat on the stone wall surrounding the water and gazed at the statue, it felt so good to be looking at a representation of divinity and enlightenment that actually had breasts. The statue exuded a formidable feminine strength, straight-backed, her left leg folded in, her right foot down on the ground, as if ready to spring into action. The only part of the statue that wasn't green were her eyes, which had been painted white, giving her a formidable gaze, and her lips, which were painted red.

The Tibetan Buddhists have a mantra that they chant to Green Tara: '*Om Tare Tuttare Ture Soha*,' which translated means, 'Om O Tara, I pray O Tara, O swift one, so be it.' By reciting Green Tara's mantra, Tibetan Buddhists are asking her for her blessing and opening themselves up to her qualities of wisdom and compassion, for the benefit of all. As we sat around the statue, in this portal of Love and kindness at the top of the world, I was struck by the notion that this was exactly what we were supposed to be doing. This was what we'd been created for. The modern, fast-paced world with its striving for material wealth and its hashtags of hate seemed so alien and wrong. In this state of being rather than doing, I was able to see things so clearly. I'd been plugged back into Love and wonder and was determined not to lose my way again.

The woman I'd helped up the mountain came over and gave me a hug.

'Thank you so much for helping me up here,' she said, with tears in her eyes. 'It's so beautiful.'

Her tearful smile filled my heart with joy.

Something More

Create your own pilgrimage

Is there a place that feels sacred to you, or a place you've heard about that's renowned for its spiritual properties? Plan a walk that will end at this place. One point of a pilgrimage is to test yourself physically. You need a certain amount of time for the walking to start working its magic. Choose a distance that would be a challenge for you. Before you set out, get clear about the purpose of your pilgrimage. Is there an issue you need help with? Are you seeking some kind of divine inspiration? Do you crave a deeper sense of connection to Something More? Would you like to dedicate your walk to someone in need? Would you like to use your pilgrimage as a show of thanks? Or maybe it could be a mixture of all of these. Getting clear on your intentions before you set out really helps to focus your mind and get the most from the experience. Take a notepad with you to jot down any thoughts or inspirations that come – and they will come, trust me. If you have to take a phone, keep it switched off. Nothing kills the pilgrimage spirit faster than incessant notification pings.

Green Tara meditation

Sitting in a comfortable position with your spine straight, take a few slow, deep, relaxing breaths, in through the nose and out through the mouth. Make sure that your belly is expanding on the in-breath and contracting on the out-breath. When you feel focused and relaxed start chanting the Green Tara mantra: 'Om Tare Tuttare Ture Soha' (pronounced: om-ta-ray-to-ta-ray-to-ray-so-ha). Green Tara embodies fearlessness and courage so this is a great mantra to chant any time you need some extra help overcoming an obstacle – whether it be internal or external. Hold the obstacle in your mind as you chant and visualise yourself channelling the courage of Green Tara as you find the strength to overcome it.

If you'd prefer a soundtrack to chant to there are many different videos of the Green Tara mantra on YouTube, so take a look through some of them and choose one that feels the right rhythm and speed for you. Once again, after your meditation is over, write any thoughts, observations or inspirations in your journal.

16

SOULMATES AND SOUL FRIENDS

Real friendship or love is not manufactured
or achieved by an act of will or intention.
Friendship is always an act of recognition.

JOHN O'DONOHUE

In his wonderful book *Anam Cara*, Irish poet, author and priest John O'Donohue writes: 'You can never love another person unless you are equally involved in the beautiful but difficult, spiritual work of learning to love yourself.' Before my spiritual quest, I had this all the wrong way around, believing that if I could get someone else to love me first, then I'd be able to love myself. As I put self-love at the heart of my spiritual practice, the neediness I used to have when it came to relationships melted away. For the first time in my adult life I enjoyed being single, revelling in the space it gave me to deepen my connection to Something More. And then, of course, when I was least expecting it, I met a guy.

I'd been invited to read an extract from my latest novel at an event at Keats House, a beautiful museum in London's Hampstead that was once home to the romantic poet John Keats. I'd got there early so I took the opportunity to have a wander round and drink in the Keats memorabilia. As I was coming up a narrow flight of stairs from the basement I walked past a man. Even though I'd never met him before, I felt a powerful jolt of recognition as my gaze met his. I felt the same jolt of recognition when he got up to read during the event. It turned out that he was one of the other writers on the bill, but I was certain I'd never encountered him on the writing circuit before. As I watched him perform his poetry I wracked my brains, trying to work out where I knew him from. As I realised that I definitely didn't know him, another thought occurred to me – maybe I was feeling this recognition because I was *supposed* to know him. When I got up to read from my book I saw him smiling at me with the same warm, knowing look. Perhaps I'd been possessed by the romantic spirit of Keats, but I found myself picturing our souls floating high above us, exchanging hugs and reminiscences while we waited for our bodies to catch up.

After the readings the poet and I got chatting and we exchanged contact details. I invited him to read at an event I was organising the following month at the Poetry Cafe in Covent Garden. When I saw him again at that event the feeling of recognition was even stronger. We started messaging each other. We gave each other nicknames. One day, when we were chatting via Messenger while I was in a supermarket queue, he let me know that he was single in such a crow-barred way that it was obvious that he really wanted me to know. When I realised this I couldn't stop grinning inanely at the checkout lady.

Then I let him know that I was single, in an equally awkward way, because I really wanted him to know too. The waters had been tentatively tested. The sense that I already knew him grew stronger and stronger. Getting to know him actually felt more like a case of getting to *re-know* him. I'd never experienced anything like it before. I'd never felt so calm and certain when it came to a guy either, and I knew that this had to be down to my new-found spiritual faith.

Before, when I'd met a guy and liked him, my excitement had come tainted with panic. *But what if I lose him,* underscored everything. If I lost him I'd lose love and therefore everything, or so it felt. The Sufi poet Rumi once wrote: 'Your task is not to seek for love, but merely to seek and find all the barriers within yourself that you have built against it.' It seems counter-intuitive to build barriers against love – after all, isn't love what we're all craving? But the paradox is, as much as we crave it, love can be a terrifying prospect because love comes hand in hand with the risk of loss, which comes arm in arm with its sidekick, pain. All of us who have loved and lost have known that searing pain, and in our darkest moments vowed 'never again'. By the time I was twenty-one I knew three things for sure: 'London Calling' by the Clash was the best rock song ever recorded; flat-pack furniture instructions are harder to crack than the Enigma code, and loving and losing another person can really hurt. Moreover, I wasn't being melodramatic with number three – I had solid evidence. I'd been devastated by my parents' marriage break-up, but the damage was all internal – an emotional implosion. Years later my dad told me that on the night he and my mum split up I sat in the living room, staring blankly at the television, 'beyond tears', as he wrote in his diary. A barrier went up inside me that night. I could practically hear it clunking into place. From that moment on love always came with the expectation of hurt and so, of course, hurt's exactly what I got. With every unrequited love or failed relationship I experienced over the next few years, my barrier was reinforced.

However, the truth is that hefting around a great barrier to love is exhausting. Instead of keeping you safe, it makes you brittle and hard and *you still end up hurting*. It can also cause you to make some truly regretful choices. It was only when I finally started to dismantle the barriers I'd built up that I was able to access true love – and by that I mean true spiritual Love. When I met the poet, the barrier I'd built as a teenager was well and truly demolished, and I felt deeply rooted in Love. Opening up myself to the possibility of loving this man didn't feel like 'betting the ranch'. If I loved him and lost him – I wouldn't lose Love. I'd never lose Love. I'd just lose him.

One night the poet and I went out for dinner in London. Afterwards, he walked me to the station and waited with me for my train. When the train came and he hugged me tightly I felt absolutely rooted in the certainty that I was exactly where I was meant to be. On our next date we were supposed to be going for a drink, but a torrential thunderstorm led to us holing up in the cosy living room of my cottage instead. We played Stevie Wonder records, ate pizza and drank apple juice. And we talked and talked. While we did so all I could think was, *I've known you forever*. He was on a similar spiritual journey to mine, having turned his back on organised religion, and it was great to compare notes about all we'd learnt. Then we meditated together and it was quite literally mind-blowing. The connection to Something More that I experienced when I meditated on my own was amplified to an extraordinary level. The 'I am' that Ken had taught me about became 'We are'. At one point I had to open my eyes to check that we were still actually sitting, cross-legged, on my living room floor. When we made love that night it felt like the first time and the thousandth time – exciting, new and wonderfully familiar all at once. Afterwards, I lay in his arms listening to the rain on the window and he whispered in my ear: 'What are you thinking?' Instead of feeling awkward or making some kind of naff joke, as I'd done in intimate situations in the past, the only thing I could think was, *I love you*. It sounds cheesy, I know, but I felt so completely and utterly connected to him in that moment that all I felt was Love – and it was a love that felt pure and healthy and without conditions.

Of course, I didn't tell him what I was thinking. Even in my blissed-out bubble I was savvy enough to know that saying 'I love you' so soon was akin to the phrase 'We need to talk', in terms of striking terror into the heart of a grown man. But the key thing was that I didn't make a wisecrack to try and push him away, because for once in my life I wasn't lying in a new man's arms feeling terrified. I had no idea what was going to happen between us but it didn't matter. I was so used to opening my heart to Love by then that it felt like the most natural thing in the world to share this Love with another soul.

As the weeks went on it felt so liberating to share my true self so freely. I saw for the first time in my life the incredible power that comes with vulnerability. During one of our long, late-night chats I told the poet that when I was a child I'd longed to be named Daisy – so badly that I'd even launched a passive-aggressive campaign against my parents, writing 'This belongs to Daisy Curham' inside every single one of my books. In response, he wrote me a poem called 'Doubtless Daisy Dance', all about celebrating love courageously. For the first time in my life, when it came to a man I was no longer plagued by doubt and fear. I'd done the work and now I was reaping the rewards. It felt so right, so predestined, so Elizabeth Gilbert in *Eat, Pray, Love*. Can you tell there's a big old *but* coming?

I want you to imagine that this book came with a soundtrack and right now you're hearing the sound of a needle being rudely ripped across my Stevie Wonder album – because a couple of months after this love story began, it came to an abrupt end. The mother of the poet's child, who'd ended their relationship a year before, found out that he'd met someone he was serious about – that is, me – and told him that she wanted him back. Their child was young. The poet and I had only known each other a couple of months – or lifetimes, depending on how you looked at it. This latest development cast a huge shadow over everything. The bottom line was that I didn't want to get in the way of a family being together. If I'm coming across here like a sickly, selfless saint, trust me, I'm not and I wasn't. Our parting of ways was messier than I'd have wished and there were moments when I hated his ex with a vengeance. I may have even written a couple of passive-aggressive Facebook posts. I had dark nights of the soul where the only prayer I could muster was 'Why?' and it caused my heart to ache. But crucially, it didn't cause my heart to break because I saw that if I were to truly walk the walk of my spiritual talk then a fundamental part of loving unconditionally was letting go unconditionally. So, I let go. With Love.

This is the real crux of the matter: our relationships are our greatest spiritual assignments, and other people are our greatest teachers, even when they hurt us – *especially* when they hurt us. So I drew upon the spiritual teachings I'd learnt in the previous couple of years to help me through the pain. I leant heavily on the Buddhist practice of letting go of attachment, which Buddha had deemed to be the route of all suffering. Inspired by Jesus's teachings, I upped my practice of loving myself and others, trying to replace thoughts of fear and anger with kindness and forgiveness (note the use of the word 'trying'; this stuff was not easy). I immersed myself in the poetry of the Sufis, using this quote from the Persian poet Hafiz to remind me of the importance of loving unconditionally: 'Even after all this time The Sun never says to The Earth, "You owe me." Look what happens with a love like that. It lights the whole sky.'

I danced, chanted, meditated and prayed the pain out of my body. Instead of wallowing in self-pity, I tried to see the hurt I was feeling as an opportunity to go deeper with my spiritual practice. I also realised that, just as when I'd lost my dog Max, the sorrow I was experiencing was in direct proportion to the joy I'd felt. So often when it comes to loss, we torture ourselves with thoughts of 'why?' But as I danced, cried, meditated and prayed my way out of the pain, I came to see that the why doesn't really matter at all. What really matters is the *how* – how you handle yourself during the loss, and how you make your way back to a place of Love.

When I'd first met the poet and experienced that deep feeling of recognition it had crossed my mind that I'd met my soulmate. Back then, I'd taken the term soulmate to mean a romantic partner who you're destined to be with, but it turns out that in spiritual circles the term has quite a different meaning. In spiritual circles a soulmate is someone you're destined to meet but for spiritual rather than romantic reasons. So, as well as a partner or lover, a soulmate could turn up in your life in the form of a sibling, parent, child or friend, or even a really irritating work colleague. The point is that soulmates come into our lives to help us learn and grow. There's also a theory that our soulmates will show up time and again over various lifetimes and in various guises, to teach us valuable lessons. I'm aware that there's absolutely no scientific proof to back up this theory but equally, I can't dispute the fact that there are certain people in my life I've felt destined to meet. And this hasn't just been with romantic partners.

A couple of years ago I moved to a place called Lewes, where I started running a weekly writing group. I instantly warmed to a woman called Sarah who came along to the first meeting, and I had the strongest gut feeling that we ought to be friends. It was really strange. Just as I'd experienced the night I met the poet in Keats House, there was something so familiar about her, even though I was certain we'd never met before. Sarah and I arranged to go for a coffee one Saturday afternoon, and the conversation was still flowing when the cafe closed. We therefore adjourned to a nearby park and carried on chatting on a bench in the evening sun. Our conversation meandered on to the subject of travel and we realised that we'd both been staying in the same region of Spain, at the same time, a couple of years previously. As I was showing her some photos from my retreat she recognised the Sufi cafe. 'I sat in that same chair and read that same book!' she exclaimed. But a stranger thing was to come. About a month later when we were having dinner together we discovered that we'd both worked in the same office back when I was twenty and Sarah was eighteen. I'd just dropped out of university and Sarah was working there for the summer before leaving to start her degree. Moreover, not only had we worked in the same office, but we'd sat in the same chair – not at the same time, I hasten to add, because I think I'd definitely have remembered her if that were the case. Sarah had, in fact, covered my job at the weekends. We'd never actually met back then, but on Monday mornings I'd come in to a set of her handwritten notes updating me on what had happened on Saturday. Now, I'm well aware that if I put a story like this in one of my novels I'd be accused of a plot twist that defied credibility. But the fact is, it happened and it's the closest I've got to proof that we are meant to meet certain people, as Sarah has gone on to become a true soul friend.

I learnt about the concept of soul friends from another friend of mine called Sammie. As soon as I met Sammie I had the same feeling I'd had with Sarah; a sense of recognition and a certain feeling that we were supposed to know each other. The night we met I noticed that Sammie was wearing a bracelet with the phrase 'Anam Cara' engraved on it and I asked her what it meant.

'Anam cara is an ancient Celtic tradition. It means soul friend,' she explained.

I was intrigued. Sammie recommended that I read *Anam Cara* by John O'Donohue. In the book, O'Donohue talks about how a soul friendship goes far deeper than ego or personality. An anam cara is a person to whom you can confess your deepest secrets; they are a spiritual guide as well as a companion. O'Donohue argues that everyone needs a soul friend; someone who sees our very essence and truly understands us. When we feel understood, we are able to lower our masks and share our true self, or our soul.

It turns out that the concept of the anam cara predates the Celts, who adopted it from the early desert Christians. The desert Christians were men and women in the third, fourth and fifth centuries who left their homes and moved to the deserts of Egypt, Syria and Palestine. They valued solitude as a way of connecting more deeply with God and sought out isolated locations, where they could find 'soul space' to be silent and

contemplate. They were pioneers of the Christian monastic tradition, usually living in simple cells. However, they also valued
deep friendship and would often share their cell with a soul
friend, to whom they would open their heart; a process they
referred to as 'exagoreusis'. The really interesting thing about
this, bearing in mind the patriarchal structure of the Christian
churches today, is that these friendships could be between men
and women, young and old, lay people and the ordained. A
key maxim of the Desert Mothers and Fathers, as they became
known, was, 'Be an example, not a law-giver.' Oh, the irony!

The theology professor and author Edward Sellner identifies
seven key characteristics of a soul friendship:

1. Great affection and depth.
2. A profound respect for each other's wisdom.
3. Common values and a shared interpretation
   of reality.
4. The ability to challenge each other when necessary.
5. Being rooted in spiritual faith.
6. Surviving separation – be it geographically or even
   through death.
7. An appreciation of solitude as well as friendship in
   order to find peace with one's self and the world.

The first thing I thought as I read about these wonderful friendships was that this is exactly what I have with my dad and my
lifelong best friend Tina. It was a relationship I longed to cultivate with others too. Spiritual friendships aren't unique to the
Christian and Celtic traditions.

In Buddhism the concept of *kalyana mittata*, meaning an
admirable or noble friend, is based on supporting each other

through shared values and the pursuit of enlightenment. In the *Upaddha Sutta* the Buddha says to his disciple Ananda:

> Admirable friendship, admirable companionship, admirable camaraderie is actually the whole of the holy life. When a monk has admirable people as friends, companions and comrades he can be expected to develop and pursue the noble eight-fold path.

This view is echoed in the Triratna Buddhist community, an international network established in 1967 with the purpose of adapting Buddhist teachings to the modern world. Sangharakshita, the founder of the community, emphasises the importance of having a group of spiritual friends with whom we can be completely honest and intimate, to help develop the virtues of generosity, compassion, forgiveness and patience.

When I first left the Christian Church one thing I really missed was this sense of spiritual community – it felt like a big drawback to choosing the 'spiritual but not religious' path. However, learning about the concept of soul friends has taught me such a valuable and positive lesson. When you put Something More at the heart of your friendships you can build your own spiritual community. In Sarah and Sammie I found two more anam caras; women I'm able to open my heart and bare my soul to. Moreover, when I reflect back on how my soul led me to them, in Sarah's case repeatedly, and the sense of recognition my soul felt upon our meeting, it only reinforces my belief in the magic of Something More.

Something More

Soul friends

Is there anyone in your life you would view as a 'soul friend'? Perhaps there's someone with whom you share a mutual understanding and respect, and whose wisdom and companionship you really treasure – a friendship that isn't affected by separation, age or gender. Think back to when you first met this person. Did you feel a sense of recognition? Write in your journal about how you could nurture this friendship further and see it as an opportunity to love. If you don't have a soul friend, write about how you might get to meet one. Do the Resting in Love (see page 34) meditation and tune in to your intuition. Note down anything it tells you to do. In the meantime, focus on being your own soul friend. Make a list of all the ways in which you can nurture your soul, deepen your faith in Something More and bring more love to the world.

Soulmates

If you have a partner or you've just started dating someone, ask yourself how you could see your relationship as a spiritual opportunity. Instead of focusing on the needs, shortcomings, fears and 'what ifs' so frequently associated with romantic love, focus on Love with a capital L. Free write your answers to the following questions in your journal to help you:

- How does your relationship provide an opportunity to tap into a greater, spiritual Love?

- How can you grow this Love and grow as a spiritual being in this Love?
- What fears need to be released in order for this Love to grow?
- What, more loving, thoughts could replace these fears?

Aching but not breaking

If you've recently experienced a break-up free write on the following questions in your journal, to help work your way back to Love:

- How can you see the break-up as a spiritual experience?
- What are you grateful for in spite of the pain?
- What needs to be let go of and forgiven?

17

MINDFULNESS AND THINKING YOURSELF HAPPY

All that we are is the result of what we have thought.

BUDDHA

You'd have to have been living in a cave for the past couple of years to not have noticed the explosion in the mindfulness movement, with countless books, courses, retreats and apps now available promoting a more mindful way of living. Mindfulness essentially means bringing your awareness back to the present moment, rather than having it hopping about all over the place, trapped in anxious or fearful projections – and in a world where mental illnesses such as anxiety and depression are on the rise, there's a growing need for the psychological support mindfulness offers. To give some indication of just how popular mindfulness has become, by 2016 over six million people had downloaded the Headspace mindfulness app. Mindfulness has proven to be so effective in helping with issues like depression and anxiety that it is even being embraced by the medical world. A trial featured in the *Journal of Consulting and Clinical Psychology* in 2013 showed that mindfulness-based cognitive therapy is just as effective at reducing the recurrence of depression as antidepressants – but with none of the side effects medication can involve. A research study published by the University of Oxford in 2013 showed that people who had taken part in the Be Mindful online course experienced a 58 per cent reduction in anxiety, a 57 per cent reduction in depression and a 40 per cent reduction in stress.

As mindfulness is embraced by the medical establishment for being a highly effective psychological tool, it's easy to forget its spiritual roots. Mindfulness originated in the Buddhist tradition, where it is known by the Pali term *sati* and seen as an essential step on the path to enlightenment and the allevi-ation of suffering. When I first moved to Lewes I discovered a Buddhist sangha (group) that met every week around the corner from my flat. I hadn't been to a Buddhist meeting since the very beginning of my spiritual quest, some five years previ-ously, but this was a very different type of Buddhism from the one practised by followers of Nicherin. This strand followed the teachings of the Vietnamese Zen Buddhist monk Thich Nhat Hanh, who is known for being a huge proponent of mindful-ness. This is what drew me to the group. Although I was so much happier than I had been at the start of my spiritual quest, I still got ambushed on a regular basis by my thoughts, and most especially my fear thoughts, and quite frankly, I was sick of it. As Mark Twain once said, 'I'm an old man and have known a great many troubles, but most of them never happened.' I was sick of wasting time and energy worrying about issues that never came to be, and wanted to free myself from the Fox News-style ticker tape of fear that so often played on a loop in my head.

The first time I went to the sangha there were about twenty people there and we all sat on chairs in a circle. We started with a reading from Thich Nhat Hanh but unlike in a church, where only a chosen few get to speak, the book was passed around the circle and we were all invited to take part, reading a couple of paragraphs each. I really liked the lack of a power structure and loved the reading. It was all about how to attain peace in the present moment. Hanh is a huge fan of the present moment because, as he states, it's really all we have. The past is over and the future is yet to come – but we spend so much time projecting backwards and forwards between the two, completely wasting the gift of the now.

Thich Nhat Hanh recommends breathing as a way of bringing ourselves back to the present moment, or rather '*mindful* breathing'. He also recommends mindful eating, listening, thinking and walking – more on which in a bit. Mindful breathing is deceptive in its seeming simplicity. You just bring your mind's attention to the in-breath and the out-breath. How hard can that be? After we'd finished the reading we did a breathing meditation together. At first my mind kept hopping about all over the place: *I wish I'd eaten more before I came out, I'm really hungry. That woman to the left of me looks a little strange – I hope she doesn't try talking to me. I wonder what inspired Neil Diamond to write 'Sweet Caroline'. When I get home I'm going to make myself some toast – or maybe a pizza. God, I'm starving.* But the sound of the bell kept pulling my attention back to my breathing. Using the bell is another technique Hanh employs to bring people back to a state of mindfulness. In his Buddhist community, Plum Village in France, a bell is sounded regularly to remind people to focus on their breathing and come back to the present moment. Every time the bell sounds, members of the community have to stop what they're doing and stand in silent contemplation for a few moments. Imagine that. Imagine if throughout your day, you had to stop working/cooking/playing music/talking/Netflix-and-chilling, and listened to a bell and focused on your breath. This may seem highly regimented but the fact is, our mind can be such a fearful, flighty thing that we need constant reminders to bring it back to a state of peace. So I breathed in and out, and in and out, and slowly but surely my mind quietened. A calm fell upon the group as we became unified through our breathing.

When our meditation ended, some fifteen minutes later, I felt completely relaxed. Then it was time for some mindful walking. I'd never come across the concept of mindful walking before, but as a great fan of walking I was eager to see what it entailed – until I saw that we had to walk around the garden in front of the building, which was completely visible to the adjacent road and footpath. Dusk was falling but sadly it wasn't nearly dusky enough to not be seen. One of the guys from the group began leading us in a long, slow procession round and round the garden – and when I say slow, I mean *really* slow. Think zombie shuffle. The point of mindful walking is very different from going on a pilgrimage. It's much less about the walking and much more about the being mindful. With every step we were meant to stop and drink in our surroundings. At first all I could think was, *Thank God I haven't lived here long and the chances of anyone I know seeing me are zero.* Then I thought, *Actually, even if I don't know them it will still be mortally embarrassing being seen trailing around a garden like a procession of zombies.* I focused on coordinating my breath with my feet, breathing in slowly on one step and out on the next. This definitely helped. Finally I was able to start paying attention to the surroundings. The grass felt lush and spongy beneath my feet, and the scent from a nearby lavender bush was intoxicating. Walking like this was a novel experience for me. I'm so used to using a walk as a means to an end or a way of sorting through any issues on my mind. It felt so strange to simply focus on the walk itself – strange but very pleasant. That was, until a passer-by saw us lurching towards her through the gloom and let out a blood-curdling scream.

After our mindful walk we came back inside for some mindful listening. This was something I really struggled with. The idea was that if any of us needed to offload, we were welcome to share how we were feeling with the rest of the group. While we were sharing our feeling, it was the rest of the group's job to listen mindfully and to not speak – not even once we'd finished talking. *What's the point of that?* I thought to myself. *What use will it be, if we're not allowed to offer any kind of advice or reassurance?* The first person began speaking – a lengthy monologue about her day. I attempted to give her my full and unbroken attention but it was really difficult. There was no real point to what she was saying – it was literally a reportage of a pretty non-eventful day. I found myself starting to think judgemental thoughts like, *She really hasn't understood the point of this* and *Do we really need to know that you decided to drive here via the A27?* However, because I was trying to be mindful, I was able to recognise that I was being judgemental and tried to listen with more compassion.

The next person to share was mourning the loss of her friend. It was very emotional listening to her speak and very difficult not to say anything once she'd finished. In fact, it felt heartless. However, the woman didn't seem to mind at all, in fact, and as she bowed to us all, her hands in prayer position, she looked hugely grateful. I didn't end up speaking that night but I did end up understanding the point of mindful listening. When you know that you're not allowed to say anything in response to someone it stops you from drifting off to mentally compose your response. This mental composing instead of fully listening is something I think we're all guilty of. I know I still am but thanks to the teachings of Thich Nhat Hanh I have become far more aware of it, and I'm able to catch and stop myself often and give the person speaking my full attention.

The most powerful and transformative lesson I learnt from the practice of mindfulness was when it came to my thoughts. One day, when I was reading about Buddha, I came across this quote from him that really stopped me in my tracks: 'All that we are is the result of what we have thought. The mind is everything. What you think you become.' What you think you become – I pondered that for a while. It was certainly true that when I thought certain thoughts they made me happy, and when I thought other thoughts they made me sad. In fact, everything I thought triggered some kind of emotion or feeling. This realisation wasn't exactly rocket science, yet it felt like a major breakthrough because I also realised that if I could learn to control my thoughts, then surely I would also be able to control my feelings.

For the next few weeks I became my own personal thought police, making a mental note of the thoughts I had that made me feel great and the ones that made me feel rubbish. Whenever I found myself spinning down in a thought spiral that made me feel bad I'd stop and ask myself two questions: firstly, *Was what I was thinking absolutely true?* and secondly, *What thought could I think instead, to make me feel better?* It was a bit hit and miss at first – it's hard to be mindful when your thought bubbles are like storm clouds – but with some concerted effort I started to see a real change. Thanks to Thich Nhat Hanh and Buddha, I was walking, breathing and thinking my way to happiness and inner peace.

Something More

Take yourself for a mindful walk

In order to walk mindfully it's best to go somewhere with as few distractions as possible, for example your back garden, the local park or a field at a time when it's quiet. Slow your pace right down and coordinate your breathing with your steps, taking one slow step on the in-breath and one slow step on the out-breath. Once you've relaxed into the rhythm and pace of your breathing, start opening your mind to your surroundings. What can you see? What can you hear? What can you smell? What can you feel? Really immerse yourself in the experience of the walk itself and enjoy being free from the need to get anywhere or do anything, other than walk mindfully. If you start getting lost in thoughts, picture them drifting up from your head and out into the sky like clouds, separate from you. Observe them drift away, then return your attention to your breathing, your steps and your surroundings.

Afterwards, record your findings in your journal. How did walking mindfully make you feel? Did you encounter any resistance at first? How did you overcome it? Did it help to coordinate your steps with your breathing?

Practise bringing a more mindful approach into everything you do, from household chores, to your work and eating. This can be a particularly powerful practice during times of stress or anxiety as it's a great way of coming out of any fearful projections and relaxing into the present moment.

Find the gap between your thoughts and feelings

Start getting into the habit of monitoring your thoughts – and how they make you feel. Take some time to note down in your journal the thoughts that cause you to experience positive emotions such as joy, peace, inspiration and unity, and the thoughts that cause you to feel negative emotions such as anger, fear, stress, regret and sorrow. Become aware of how your thoughts create your perception of the world and whether it is a loving or fearful place.

Once you have this awareness it's easier to find a gap between your thoughts and the feelings or emotions they will create. So, for example, you might catch yourself thinking, *I wish I was as clever as my brother*, a thought that traditionally makes you feel stupid and inadequate. Before you spiral down into those feelings, ask yourself what you could think instead to make you feel happier. For example, *Academic excellence is not a reflection of a person's worth*. Check in with your body. How does this new thought make you feel? Is there anything else you could think to make you feel even better, for example *I love and accept myself* or *I am a gifted human being*? Once again, check in with yourself and see how these new thoughts make you feel.

If you fall out with someone and feel yourself spiralling down into bitterness or anger, stop your thoughts of accusation and blame, and ask yourself what you could think instead to make you feel better. *She's such a bitch* could be changed to *She really hurt me*, for example, then *She really hurt me* could be changed to *She has a lot of issues that make her lash out*. Keep asking yourself what you could think instead until you've worked your way up a ladder of thoughts to a place of happiness and peace. In this scenario, you might work your way up to a thought like *I forgive her and release my anger.*

18

SPIRITUAL TOOLS FOR TOUGH TIMES

This, too, will be for the best.

NAHUM OF GIZMO

Seeing my son grow into a kind, sensitive and funny young man has been the greatest privilege of my life, so when he became seriously ill a few months after we moved to Lewes, it felt as if my world was ending. When I say seriously ill, I mean hospital ill; not-sure-he's-going-to-make-it ill. Our world was shaken like a snow globe, and pieces of it were cascading all around, settling into a harsh new routine. There were hospital visits, meetings with medical staff, a diet of black coffee and jelly beans. As I watched my strapping twenty-year-old son disintegrate before my eyes, I felt a fierce pain tugging at the invisible umbilical cord that has always bonded us – and for the first time since I'd embarked on my spiritual quest, my new-found faith in Something More was shaken to the core. Initially, I was too shocked, tired and distracted to remember to do things like meditate. Then, after a particularly stressful day at the hospital, when it crossed my mind that maybe I ought to pray, I was filled with anger. Exactly who would I be praying to? The kind of god/creative force/universal energy that might take my son away from me? The kind of god that allowed thousands to die needlessly every single day? The kind of god who'd taken my friend Michelle after a lengthy battle with leukaemia just three years previously, at the age of thirty-four – and might now take my son at the age of twenty? Why the hell should I pray to someone or something that was capable of such cruelty? This crisis of faith made the situation even more terrifying. I felt completely and utterly alone.

However, in spite of all this, a safety net of love gathered around me. The night my son was admitted to hospital I texted one of my new friends to let her know what had happened. It was the middle of the night and she didn't have a car, but she got her friend to drive up to the hospital, some seventeen miles from Lewes. The first I knew about this was when I got a text from her at one in the morning: 'We're out in the car park in case you need a chat/hug/lift home ps: we also have chocolate and a flask of coffee. xxxx'.

I was absolutely gobsmacked. I'd only known this friend for a few months, and I'd only met her friend once, yet they hadn't hesitated to go out into the cold in the dead of night and drive miles to sit in a car park, just in case I needed them. When I stumbled out of the hospital at two in the morning and practically fell into the car, I don't think I've ever been so glad to see someone. In the weeks that followed my family also formed a safety net via text messages, calls and visits. My faith in Love was semi-restored, so I began to pray and I clung to the faintest of hopes that something might be listening.

In the middle of this dark time, my dad sent me a letter. He sends me lots of letters and usually there will be a postcard inside the envelope too, on which he will have written some kind of spiritual quote. Normally I love these quotes and find them incredibly uplifting. True to form, this letter also included a postcard, but this time, initially at least, the quotes he'd written made me nothing but angry. They were: 'This too shall pass' and 'This, too, will be for the best.' When you read phrases like these after a bad day at the office or when you've just been soaked by a rain shower they're reassuring. *Oh yes*, you say to yourself, *Of course this will pass. Silly me for getting so stressed*. But when you read them when it feels as if the worst is about to happen, they can seem like heartless taunts.

But what if it never passes? was my first thought when I read the card. *What if my son dies and I spend the rest of my life in mourning? And how the hell is this too for the best?* I went for an angry walk, hiking on the Downs like a woman possessed. As I pushed myself higher and further my anger started to fade. I knew enough from previous experience to recognise the truth in 'This too shall pass.' I thought of the time when my partner Steve was told he was going to die from cancer and I truly believed I'd never feel joy again; that the pain and fear we were experiencing would never end. But they did. And during the seven years since I'd felt so much joy, and so had Steve, who was healthy, alive and miraculously cancer free. Everything passes – even the deepest pain – especially if you remember to return to your faith in Love. I knew this and I clung to it as I hiked my way across the hills.

However, I still really struggled with the second quote my dad had sent me: 'This, too, will be for the best.' How was my son's illness for the best? How was the pain he was in for the best? How was the anguish his loved ones were feeling for the best? As hard as I searched, I couldn't find the answer. So I thought back to that other dark time in my life, when Steve was ill, and asked myself how that had been for the best. At first I couldn't think of anything. *Ha ha!* I thought as I marched up yet another hill. *It's all a load of old bollocks, Dad!* But then I remembered the unofficial mantra I'd been left with after Steve's illness – one that always popped into my head whenever I caught myself getting stressed about something silly like a burst pipe or a parking fine: *Chill out – no one's dying.* The dark time had given me a much healthier perspective on things. That was definitely for the best. But this time, someone might actually die. *My son* might die. Clearly this mantra didn't work for everything.

Had anything else about Steve's cancer diagnosis been for the best? I wracked my brains and finally found an answer. His apparent death sentence had given me an opportunity to love; *really selflessly, soulfully, spiritually love* another person through my actions as well as my words. The months we spent together facing down death in the dark shadow of his diagnosis bonded us for life. There were the internet searches for miracle cures, the weird and wonderful food – the turmeric and black pepper, spirulina and green tea that had moved into our kitchen cupboards, giving sugar, fat and alcohol the boot – the tears, the laughter, the sanity-saving gallows humour, the back-rubs, the heartfelt conversations, and the Valentine's Day we spent in bed because he was still so exhausted from surgery. It all felt like such a privilege, looking back on it, to have been pushed to the edge with another human being like this – to have been cracked wide open so that Love could flood in. The closeness we'd experienced during that time had been so much for the best, but it was only hindsight that was allowing me to see it. Then I realised the importance of the two little words at the heart of the quote. It didn't say that this too *is* for the best, but that this too *will be* for the best, the implication being that only time allows us to see the light in the darkness and the lessons in the pain.

In his book *The Problem of Pain*, C. S. Lewis wrote: 'God whispers to us in our pleasures, speaks in our conscience, but shouts in our pain.' The problem is that the voice of Love – even when it's shouting – can so often be drowned out by our fears. As I followed the path back downhill, back home, I could feel the spirit of Something More shouting at me, its messages of love and hope echoing around the velvety green hills of the Downs.

When I got back home I texted my dad.

'Where did you get "This, too, will be for the best" from?'

'Nahum of Gizmo,' came his reply. 'Just another Irishman I met down the pub.'

Actually, Nahum of Gizmo was a first-century Jewish scholar. It is said that on every occasion, no matter how horrible, he exclaimed: '*Gam zu le-tobah!*' (This, too, will be for the best.) He must have been a really popular guy. I can just picture him now, bearded and robed, popping up every time someone got attacked on the way to the bazaar, or had their camel stolen, exclaiming, 'This, too, will be for the best!' – before being chased out of town. Apparently, though, he didn't just talk about everything being for the best, but lived it too. When he reached old age and his hands and feet became paralysed, Nahum was able to see the best in his situation and rejoice in his ailments. I wasn't able to rejoice in my son's illness but, thanks to Nahum of Gizmo and my dad, I was able to see how, at a later date, I might be able to find a way in which it had been for the best – and that in itself brought some bitter-sweet solace.

My son slowly but surely began to recover, but I was finding it hard to shake off a hangover of fear. Family and friends recommended that I get some counselling, but I instinctively knew where I'd find the healing I needed – on the dance floor. So I took myself off to a 5 Rhythms class in Brighton. 5 Rhythms is a dance practice devised by an American dance teacher named Gabrielle Roth. After a childhood in the Catholic Church and education system, Roth had been left with a legacy of guilt linked to sin and sexuality. It was only during the times when she lost herself in dance during her college years that she felt free from this guilt. After leaving college she began running dance-therapy classes, and that's when she started seeing the potential for dance as a spiritual practice. Having always previously struggled with the concept of the Holy Spirit, she had the light-bulb moment realisation that the Holy Spirit was life force itself (the same thing as the Great Spirit of the Native Americans, the *prana* of the Ancient Indians and the *chi* of the Chinese).

Roth figured that if she could get people to come back into their bodies, connect to their breathing, and fully embrace the potential of their life force, her dance classes would become holy work; a way for people to 'sweat their prayers'. As a result, she developed 5 Rhythms. Her class pretty much does what it says on the tin. During the class, the music is divided into five categories according to rhythm. For the first twenty minutes or so, the rhythm is 'flowing'; music with a gentle pace, allowing the dancers to ground themselves and find their way into their bodies and the melody. Then the rhythm of the music goes up a notch into 'staccato'. The tracks played in this section will have a punchier beat – think dance tunes or African drumming. Then the music moves into 'chaos'; hard-core dance tracks, where everyone can really let loose. After chaos comes 'lyrical', where the music is light, whirly and floaty. Finally, there is 'stillness'. The music becomes super-slow and meditative, and the dance becomes inward and almost trance-like. In a nutshell, going to a 5 Rhythms class is like experiencing a deep meditation – at a rave.

The class I'd found took place every Wednesday night in a 900-year-old church in Brighton, all vaulted stone ceilings and stained glass windows, the only illumination being flickering candlelight. The wooden pews had all been pushed to the sides of the hall, leaving a huge space in the middle for dancing. I went and sat on one of the pews and took off my coat and shoes. A huge golden sculpture of Jesus looked down mournfully from the Cross he'd been nailed to above the altar. Instinctively, I felt a twinge of guilt. I'd never danced in a church before. Was it disrespectful? The music started and people began warming up. There was quite a crowd – fifty people at least, with men and women of all ages.

The thing I love most about 5 Rhythms is that you can completely lose yourself in the dance. There's no instruction from the teacher, who really plays more of a DJ role, and you don't have to dance with anyone else – unless you want to. As I dropped down out of my mind and into my body I felt myself letting go. As the tempo climbed through flow and staccato I started reliving the events of the previous couple of months, but this time, instead of taking a trip on fear's merry-go-round inside my head, I was able to dance out my fears on to the floor. I became completely immersed in my own little bubble, the other dancers being just a background blur. The rhythm of the music ramped up to chaos, and after weeks of keeping it together and trying to stay strong, I allowed myself to basically let go, leaping, stomping and shaking my way out of my pain.

At one point I looked up at the sculpture of Jesus and had the blinding realisation that what we were doing wasn't disrespectful at all. While Christianity seemed so intent on fixating on Jesus's death, we were celebrating life – and it felt so good. I raised my arms to Jesus in thanks, for the lessons he came to teach us about how to live and more importantly, how to love. I imagined the golden sculpture releasing himself from the Cross and leaping down to join us in our celebratory dance. The thought brought tears to my eyes. Then the music slowed to lyrical. I closed my eyes and finally faced my fear. My son had recovered but what if, at some point in the future, I were to lose him? Life can be so scary, so random. You never know what shock twist might be waiting for you on the next page. As I swayed softly to the music I imagined handing this, my worst fear, over to God – whoever or whatever God might be. 'Please take care of him,' I prayed silently. I pictured my son being bathed in a golden, protective light and the relief I felt was intense. The responsibility for his life didn't all rest on me. I could call on the power of Something More to help take care of him. For a brief moment in time, I experienced what the Buddha had advised was the key to an end to suffering; I was letting go of the strongest attachment I would ever have in my life – the attachment to my son. The music melted into stillness, and so did my body and mind. I stood motionless, my hands on my heart, every cell in my body dancing with Love and gratitude.

This feeling of gratitude stayed with me for days after and I felt the urgent need to give thanks in some kind of spiritual capacity. So the following Sunday I went to church. I hadn't attended a church service since I'd lived in the village, but my experience at the dance class had reminded me how much I'd got from Jesus's teachings. Besides, not all churches were as old school in their views of women and sexuality as the one I'd joined. I now lived right next door to the vibrant melting pot that is Brighton. If I was going to find a progressive brand of Christianity anywhere surely it would be there. So I did a bit of online research and decided on a church called St Peters.

When I walked inside the church that Sunday morning my first thought was, *This is like being at a gig.* The place was huge and a rock band was playing on a stage at the front. The acoustics created by the high ceiling were amazing. A large crowd of people was standing at the back of the church, chatting, obviously having a catch-up before the service began. I headed for the chairs. Fear told me to sit in an empty row, tucked away almost out of sight behind a huge pillar, but suddenly my intuition kicked in. It had spotted a woman wearing a beautiful bright yellow top, and it was telling me in no uncertain terms to go and sit by her. So I did. As the woman carried on chatting away with her family I felt a little bit awkward and embarrassed, but mostly I felt OK because I knew that I hadn't come to church that day to win some kind of popularity contest. I'd come to say thank you.

I sat back and gave a silent prayer of gratitude for my son's return to health. The crowd filed in from the back and the band cranked it up a notch or two. After about half an hour of music, one of the church leaders got up to speak. He was welcoming and warm and told us to say 'Hi' to the person sitting next to us. So I said hello to the woman in the yellow jumper and it turned out that she lived just a few minutes' walk away from me. 'I can't believe it,' she exclaimed. 'I've been coming to this church for months now and you're the first person I've met from Lewes.' What were the chances? *Erm, I think you'll find that I told you to sit there*, my intuition said knowingly. *You need to learn to trust me.* Little did I know that this was only the start of what was to become a morning of miracles.

The church leader then introduced the guest speaker, a pastor from Washington DC called Mark Batterson. He too was instantly likeable and he gave a great talk all about the power of prayer. The talk was based on his book *The Circle Maker*, which got its name from a Jewish legend about a sage called Honi, who lived just outside Jerusalem in the first century BC. During his lifetime a terrible drought was threatening to wipe out an entire generation – the generation right before Jesus – and people were starting to give up hope with God. But not Honi, who drew a circle on the ground with his staff, got inside the circle and began to pray: 'Lord of the universe, I swear before Your great name that I will not move from this circle until You have shown mercy upon Your children.' Apparently, all who were present that day were awestruck by the intensity with which Honi prayed. This was no wishy-washy, 'Dear God, if it's not too much trouble please could you maybe …' prayer. This was a soul-deep, mean it with every fibre of your body prayer – and it was immediately answered. It started to rain, and continued raining until the drought was over and the generation before Jesus was saved.

Batterson went on to talk about how reading about Honi had changed his whole attitude to prayer. He listed examples from his own life where he'd circled his prayers like Honi. He didn't mean that he'd literally drawn a circle in the sand and refused to leave it, but that he'd prayed with the same boldness and fervour – and with the same conviction that his prayer would be answered. He urged us all to pray similarly. 'God is for us,' he reminded us. 'God wants to answer our prayers.' I did my usual thing of mentally translating 'God' into 'Love'. Love wants to help us but – and here's the really important bit – in a way that is in accordance with Love. *Thy will be done.*

Batterson talked about how our prayers aren't always answered when or how we might expect. I thought of my own most recent and fervent prayers – that my son would return to full health. I'd prayed so desperately for my son's recovery, and when it hadn't come immediately I'd felt so disheartened. But now, with the benefit of hindsight, I was able to see how my prayers had been more than answered. As I made that realisation I felt overwhelmed with yet more gratitude.

When the service ended I started chatting to the woman in the yellow jumper again and asked her what she did for a living. 'I go into schools recommending books for students to read,' she told me. I laughed. 'That's funny, because I write books for children and teenagers.' She stared at me in disbelief before saying that we'd have to meet up for a coffee. Then the real miracle happened – it turned out that the living down the road from each other and having career paths that crossed was only a warm-up. The woman mentioned that she hadn't been to church much lately because her husband had been diagnosed with brain cancer. I caught my breath at yet another weird coincidence.

'My ex-boyfriend had melanoma in the brain,' I told her.

She gasped. 'That's exactly what my husband has. And the prognosis isn't good.'

I felt shivers running down my spine. 'It was the same for my partner,' I told her, 'but he's been cancer free for eight years now.'

I felt hope flowing from my heart into hers and she grabbed me in a hug. Then she introduced me to her husband and daughter and, as I shared the anti-cancer dietary and lifestyle tips that Steve and I had discovered eight years previously, I knew without a shadow of a doubt that we were experiencing a miracle. It was humbling and awe-inspiring in equal measure.

'I can't believe that you ended up sitting next to me,' the woman kept saying.

I thought back to how I'd wanted to sit somewhere else, on my own, but my inner guidance had pulled me over to her. We exchanged numbers and later she sent me this message: 'You were like the answer to so many deep mutterings in my heart – needing to connect and click with someone in church, feeling so isolated dealing with my husband's illness and the last three years of trauma. Then there you were, like an angel, understanding all those mumblings! Incredible. And you write for young adults too! Children's literature is my thing!'

And now, finally, I was able to understand the meaning of the Nahum of Gizmo quote and see how even the most terrible things can be for the best, *at least in some respects*, because they give us an opportunity to reach out to other people who are experiencing the same pain. They give us an opportunity to say to those people: 'I see you, I understand you and I will help you,' and through doing so, our own pain is alchemised into love and we find our way to the crack where the light gets in.

Something More

Pray for a miracle

When things go badly wrong it can be very easy to forget – or refuse – to pray. Anger, fear and stress can all get in the way. However, as Catholic monk, writer and theologian Thomas Merton wrote: 'Prayer and love are really learnt in the hour when prayer becomes impossible and your heart turns to stone.' When things are so bad that prayer feels impossible, *pray anyway*. Force yourself on to your knees and turn your troubles over to Love. It doesn't matter if you yell, sob or scream your prayer, *pray anyway*. It doesn't matter if you think praying is completely pointless, *pray anyway*. As well as praying for the inner strength and peace to get you through your ordeal, don't forget to pray for a miracle. I can honestly say that every time I've prayed for a miracle I've got one. Often, the miracle doesn't show up exactly how I'd imagined it to – sometimes it can be dramatically different – but it always happens, and the miracle always transforms fear into Love.

Breathe your way to peace

Meditation can be a superpower when times are hard, providing you with a welcome oasis of peace in the eye of the storm. However, like prayer, meditating can be so hard to do when your head is filled with fear. Use mindful breathing as a way of coming back into your body and into the present moment. Place one hand over your belly and feel it expand as you breathe in. In your mind say, 'This is my in-breath.' Feel your belly go in as you breathe out and silently say, 'This is my out-breath.' The joy of this simple, mindful meditation is that you can do it anywhere – on a train, in a hospital waiting room – wherever and whenever you're feeling stressed. Try to remember to do it. It really can make a huge difference.

Let go and let Love

Once you've brought yourself back to the present moment through your mindful breathing close your eyes, if you haven't already, and picture yourself as a wave in a golden sea of Love. Rest in this Love for a moment, then visualise yourself letting go of the cause of your stress – letting go with Love and into Love. Trust that the vast ocean of Love that flows through all of creation will take care of things. Keep breathing slowly and deeply. Keep resting. And keep trusting that all will be well.

Release attachment to outcome

If you are clinging on to the desire for a particular outcome, visualise yourself letting go of this now. Keep breathing slowly and deeply. Watch your desired outcome drifting away from you, into the sea of Love. Relinquish control – it was never yours to control anyway. Feel your body fill with the peace that truly letting go brings.

How will this, too, be for the best?

If you're going through a dark night of the soul, ponder Nahum of Gizmo's words and free write your answers to the following questions:

- How could your current situation also one *day* be seen as being for the best?
- What benefits do you think hindsight could bring?
- Where is the opportunity to bring, be and find Love in this situation?

19

FORGIVE THE FOOKER

An eye for an eye makes the whole world blind.

GANDHI

One major stumbling block that I continued to experience on my path to inner peace was forgiveness – or rather, the lack of it. There's a saying that I've seen variously attributed to Jesus, Buddha and Alcoholics Anonymous: 'Not being able to forgive someone is like drinking poison and hoping that they'll die.' Regardless of who actually said it, I could relate to it. I was still having trouble forgiving my ex-husband. It would have been so much easier if we hadn't had a child together, but when you have a child with someone you're bonded for life and there's the endless potential to keep picking at the scab of your break-up. You therefore get sucked into a downwards spiral; they say or do something that presses your buttons, you react angrily – either in person or in your

head – you feel rubbish, and this is quadrupled if you're supposed to be on some kind of spiritual path because the thoughts
you're having most definitely aren't loving. So, not only do you
end up poisoning yourself with resentment, but you feel like a
horrible human being too. Great.

Luckily, Star from the Spanish retreat (see page 171)
offered one-to-one coaching sessions via Skype. So I booked
an appointment and offloaded my woes. When I'd finished
there were a couple of seconds' silence, then she replied in
her deadpan Northern accent: 'I guess you're just going to
have to forgive the fooker.' At this point we both cracked
up laughing and I instantly felt better – because Star wasn't
swearing for the fun of it, but was acknowledging exactly
how hard true forgiveness can be. Something that can
prevent people from forgiving is the misconception that forgiving is condoning. It definitely isn't. In a sense, forgiveness
has nothing to do with what the perpetrator has done and
everything to do with you and how you choose to react.
When people forgive the killers of their loved ones they're
obviously not condoning the act of murder, but choosing
to let go of their bitterness and anger. Rather than being a
sign of weakness, forgiveness requires huge inner strength.
Sometimes it can be so hard that you need to break it down
into stages, with the first stage simply being the *willingness*
to forgive. Sometimes we need to spend days, weeks or even
months working on the willingness part before we can move
on to actually forgive. I was definitely willing, though. In
fact, I'd spent huge chunks of time in the years since we'd
spilt up genuinely thinking I had forgiven my ex – but then
something would happen between him and my son and back
it would all rush again.

'What would you have missed if you hadn't met your ex?' Star asked.

My head filled with sarcastic responses, but my desire to achieve peace outweighed my desire to be a bitch. The first response was instant and easy; I would have missed having my son – the biggest gift I'd ever been given. Then other, more unexpected answers filled my mind. I would have missed the magical moments the three of us shared as a family in the early days of our relationship. I would have missed a lot of silliness and laughter. I would have missed the moments of closeness and connection, when the jagged edges of our damaged souls seemed to fit together so perfectly. It was a powerful exercise. And the more I meditated on my answers to the question, the more I realised that it was actually possible to love your so-called enemy.

Forgiveness comes up time and again in the Christian faith. It's a key tenet of the Lord's Prayer – which Jesus taught in the Sermon on the Mount as being *the* way to pray. As a child I chanted, 'Forgive us our trespasses, as we forgive those who trespass against us', parrot-fashion in school assemblies without having a clue what it meant, but now I could see that it was one of the most essential and transformative of all the Christian teachings. *Loving our enemy wouldn't be possible if we weren't able to forgive them first.* Forgiveness is the gateway to the hardest and most transformative love of all.

In the original version of the New Testament, written in Greek, the word that is translated as forgiveness literally means 'let it go'. Letting go is also a key teaching in Buddhism – in fact Buddha believed that our inability to let go of attachments is at the root of all human suffering. It's easy to see how not letting go of anger and resentment is bad for us. I remember watching an interview with a woman whose child had been brutally murdered many years previously. It was clear from what she said in the interview that she was still eaten up with anger at what had happened to her son. It oozed from her words. It was also etched into her haggard face. In contrast, I remember seeing an interview with a man who lost his daughter in an IRA bombing. As soon as his daughter was murdered he appeared on TV to say that, as a Christian, he forgave her killers. He went on to set up a charity in his daughter's memory, and when I saw him interviewed a few years later, I was struck by the sense of calm and peace he exuded. I *wanted* the calm and peace he exuded.

So I started using prayer and meditation as a way of trying to achieve forgiveness. I prayed for my ex-husband and his happiness and peace. I prayed for his relationship with our son – that it would be strong and content. I prayed that their time spent together would be full of laughter, love and fun. When I first started praying, my inner voice had a field day. *He doesn't deserve that. You're the one who should have a great relationship with your son, not him. Blah ... blah ... self-righteousness ... self-pity ... blah.* But I kept on praying anyway, and when I meditated I would visualise myself letting go of any residual anger. It was a powerful combination. As I kept on letting go of negative thoughts, space was created for more positive and healing thoughts to come in. I also recited the Hawaiian *Ho'oponopono* prayer: 'I'm sorry, please forgive me, thank you, I love you.'

Turning things around like this and asking for his forgiveness was a powerful exercise – and when I say powerful I mean really hard, at least at first. All I could think was, *I don't need to ask him to forgive me.* But within minutes I felt a real breakthrough.

The fact is, we all mess up, we all hurt each other and we all need forgiveness. Acting like some kind of saintly martyr does no one any favours, least of all you.

Another thing I learnt during this time is that we need to see forgiveness as a state of mind rather than the occasional act. The fact is, every single day we are faced with things and people we need to forgive – anything from an eejit pushing in front of us in a queue, to a friend or loved one hurting us or, on a larger scale, to governments bringing in policies you find abhorrent. I was severely tested on this last one when the UK voted for Brexit. Then I met my dad for a pub lunch.

'How could people vote for this?' I asked him.

I was expecting him to start raging about other people's stupidity but instead he put the focus back on me.

'You need to come back to a place of Love,' he told me. 'Don't let fear uproot you.'

He helped me to see how the people who voted for Brexit – and the politicians, press and media that encouraged them – weren't the only ones coming from a place of fear. I was too. It wasn't pretty. It wasn't helpful. And it certainly wasn't healthy. A few days after our lunch I received a letter from my dad, in which he said this:

Well, you certainly reminded me of a (younger) me the other day – the anger, the righteous anger! – the disillusionment – despair. Been there. Many times. And it took me *years* to get well. Yes, I'm saying, this is not a good way to be. The world is going to keep on giving us opportunities to re-enact this anger/despair scenario and we can end up like a guy who keeps scratching at a wound – it *never* gets better.

As soon as I read his words I thought of the wound I'd scratched for years over my ex. My dad was right – it wasn't a good way to be. The only way to get 'well', as he put it, was through compassion and forgiveness. I patched up things with a friend I'd fallen out with over Brexit, stopped ranting on my social media and doubled down on fighting the fear with Love instead. I began writing a novel telling the story of a Syrian refugee. It was time to put my spiritual money where my mouth was. It was time to become a spiritual activist.

A few months later, Donald Trump was elected US President. Just as with Brexit, people began falling out left, right and centre. This time, however, I was able to refrain from adding to the anger and hate – in public at least – and published a blog post called 'Let Love Be Your Leader'. In the post I shared the quote from my dad's letter and urged people to see the news as a massive call to action to add to the love in the world, not the hate. As well as my dad, I quoted Dr Martin Luther King, Jr, Jesus and Gandhi. 'We need to rise up and show up and speak up for Love,' I wrote. 'And we need to do it with grace, not fear.' Friends started sharing the post and it got hundreds, then thousands, of views. I started receiving messages from Americans, all of them positive. This one, from a woman named Rochelle, sums up the general theme: 'This has been more helpful to me than anything I've read in months. I can feel the healing begin already.'

Love is helpful and healing, especially when it comes in its most potent form – that of forgiveness. When it comes to bringing about change we need to forgive first, then take action. If we don't, we spiral into fear and judgement and remain divided. Forgiveness opens hearts, minds and doors and transforms the hateful and the painful into Love.

Something More

Stepping stones to forgiveness

Because forgiveness can be so hard it can really help to break it down into the following steps.

Think of someone you need to forgive, then:

1. Acknowledge that by forgiving them you're not condoning their behaviour, but simply letting go of your anger. There's a big difference.

2. Come up with a healthy way of expressing your anger towards them. If you aren't able to tell the person face to face, write them a letter. If you're not able to send the letter it doesn't matter – write it anyway. Writing down your feelings can be a great way of getting them out of your body.

3. Physically release your anger. If you've written a letter, burn it* or rip it up and flush it down the toilet, or throw it into a river or the sea. Go on a run or hike and visualise yourself discarding your anger en route, the way a snake sheds an old skin. Dance or shake your anger out of your body.

4. Once you feel you've dislodged your anger it's time to let it go. Ask yourself if you're willing to forgive. That's all you need in the first instance – the

---

* Do be careful if you choose to burn your letter. When I did this once I accidentally set fire to the roller blind in my kitchen, which didn't really help my spiritual well-being at all.

willingness to let go. Use the meditation below to help you move into forgiveness.

Forgiveness meditation

Sit in a comfortable upright position and breathe in slowly through your nose and out through your mouth, feeling your stomach expand on the in-breath and contract on the out-breath.

When you're feeling relaxed, focus on your heart and visualise a golden ray of love pouring from it. See that love filling the room. Then picture the person you want to forgive sitting in front of you. Visualise the love from your heart pouring into theirs. If it becomes difficult, focus on your breathing, slowly in and out. Picture any angry or painful thoughts floating from your mind and up into the sky. See them separate from you. Know that you are not your thoughts. Breathe in the freedom that this gives you. Breathe out and let the thought go. Come back to visualising the golden light of love pouring from your heart. What happens as you picture it flowing into the person you need to forgive? Do you notice any changes in them? Do you notice any changes in you? Keep breathing slowly and deeply. Keep letting go of all thoughts. Keep picturing the love filling up the room. Let this Love lift you higher and higher, to a place free from judgement, spite, anger and pain. Look down on the events that have happened between you, as if you're watching a drama being played out by egos, driven by fear. Watch it objectively, from the safety of Love. Feel grateful that you're able to choose Love, when others aren't. Know that by choosing

Love and forgiveness you are being the light of the world – a shining example of how to live in peace. Know that the ripple effects from your forgiveness will reach far and wide. Know also that they will set you free.

IN THE END . . .

The truth is, none of us knows exactly why we are here or how the universe came to be. The only thing I know for sure is the Something More I've experienced over the past seven years and the lessons these experiences have taught me. When I remember to choose Love, my fears fade away. When I sit in silence and let go, I experience a feeling of well-being that defies description. When I pray for help and wisdom, I'm gifted with fortuitous 'coincidences'. When I allow my intuition to guide me, I make the best choices. When I open my eyes to the wonders of the world, I feel awash with gratitude. When I come into my body through yoga, walking or dance, I reconnect with my soul. When I'm mindful of my thoughts, my thoughts lead me to peace. When I'm finally able to forgive, I'm set free.

I also developed a set of tools or, as I like to call them, 'spiritual superpowers', that helped me through some of the darkest days of my life. Through it all I've come to realise that when it comes to inner joy and peace, there are many different

paths to the same destination. I've also realised that the simpler
you can keep your path, the better. I don't want to pollute my
inner peace by judging others when I could be loving them –
however hard that might sometimes be. I want to focus on the
Love that unites not the fear that divides – and not just for personal reasons. I think the world is crying out for more love and
unity. The environmental crisis, the refugee crisis, the mental
health crisis, the politics of hate and the fake news, all are signs
of a seeping toxicity. Humanity has succumbed to fear on a
global scale. But just as our individual lives can be transformed
by choosing Love over fear, the world can too. If enough of us
are prepared to be activists for Love, we can bring about real
and lasting change, for ourselves, each other and the planet.

Some people might criticise me for cherry-picking spiritual
teachings from different faiths to guide me. The unwritten rule
seems to be that you can't follow someone's teachings unless
you're a fully paid-up member of their religion. But this makes
no sense to me. For a start, there are so many contradictions
within the teachings of certain religions that it's almost impossible to subscribe to all of them. My rule of thumb when it
comes to spiritual teachings is this: *Is it loving? Is it simple? Is it
non-discriminatory?*

My dad and I went for a pub lunch the other day and, as
usual, we got talking about all things spiritual. 'I might not be
a Christian any more,' my dad said, 'but Jesus, he's my guy.'
We then went on to talk about the Bhagavad Gita, Rumi and
Heschel – a spiritual smorgasbord to go with our fish and chips.
It was wonderful. My advice would be to feast on the teachings
that bring you closer to Love and help you to feel free – whatever
they might be. One of the Buddha's last teachings was, 'Be a
lamp to yourself. Be your own confidence. Hold to the truth

within yourself as the only truth.' He urged people to work hard
at their spiritual practice, to find out what was true for them,
and not to cling to the teachings of others – including his. I
hope that this book inspires you to go on your own quest for
Something More, and that the Love you find within yourself
and others and all around transforms, liberates and empowers
you. Above all, I hope that one day we're all able to experience
the heaven on Earth that Rumi describes below:

> Out beyond ideas of wrong-doing and right-doing, there is
> a field. I'll meet you there. When the soul lies down in that
> grass, the world is too full to talk about. Ideas, language, even
> the phrase 'each other' don't make any sense.

I look forward to meeting you, out in that field.

ACKNOWLEDGEMENTS

This book was seven years in the living and, as my life started to be transformed for the better by all I was discovering, I became overwhelmed by the desire to share it with others so that they might benefit too. I'm therefore eternally grateful to editor extraordinaire, Anna Steadman, for believing in this book in its roughest, rawest form, and for all at Piatkus for making this most personal of writing dreams come true. HUGE thanks also to Jane Willis for being such a brilliant and supportive agent.

I owe a massive debt of thanks to all of the people I encountered on my 'spiritual misfit's search for meaning' but most especially I am grateful to the following people for all they have taught me: Charlotte Baldwin – thank you for inspiring me with your own spiritual transformation. Stuart Berry – thank you for introducing me to the wonders of Reiki. Ken Ryan – thank you for showing me how yoga should be. Maggie Whiteley – thank you for teaching me how to 'forgive the fooker' – the hardest, most transformational lesson of all. To everyone at Cortijo Romero – thank you for creating such a beautiful, life-changing retreat. Pip, Ruth and Altair – thank you for teaching me how to dance like Rumi. Ditto, divinest of feminines, Susie Heath. And to my other dancing queen and Insta-inspiration, Kimberly Wyatt, I hope we get to dream and do together again someday. Maddy Elruna – thank you for helping me retrieve the lost part of me. Lexie Bebbington – thank you for being such a constant source of wisdom and love. To my beautiful band of anam caras – Tina McKenzie, Sammie Venn, Sarah Walton, Sara Starbuck, Pearl Bates – how lucky am I to have you as soul sisters on this journey! Thank you to Tony Leonard and the rest of the Snowdrop Writers for being so supportive and encouraging when this book was in its infancy. Thank you to Aaron Daniel, for making this doubtless daisy dance and to Steve Rockett, for 'rippling' me away from fear on a regular basis, and to Steve O'Toole, for everything.

Massive love and thanks to my beautiful sister-sisters, Alice and Bea, my wonderful son and my number one niece, Katie.

And last but not least, thank you to my parents for making me 'just say no' to religion as a kid, leaving me free to create my own spiritual journey.